Philip Ridley was born in the East End of London and studied pa...   As a writer
his cre...   ...cluding
Krindle...   ...the Smarties Prize, *Kasper
in the Glitter* (1994), nominated for the Whitbread Prize,
and *Scribbleboy* (1997), shortlisted for the Carnegie
Medal – and two pieces for younger children. His stage
plays are *The Pitchfork Disney* (1991), *The Fastest Clock
in the Universe* (1992), which won the Meyer–Whitworth
Prize, a *Time Out* Award, and both the Critics' Circle
and the *Evening Standard* Theatre Awards for Most
Promising Playwright, *Ghost from a Perfect Place* (1994),
Vincent River (2000) and three plays for young people:
Fairytaleheart (Hampstead Theatre, 1998), *Sparkleshark*
(Royal National Theatre, 1999) and *Brokenville* (2001),
which received a Fringe First nomination at the Edinburgh
Festival. His short film, *The Universe of Dermot Finn*
(1988), was followed by his screenplay for *The Krays*
(1990), winner of the *Evening Standard* British Film of
the Year Award, and the cult classic *The Reflecting Skin*
(1990), which won eleven international awards and was
voted one of the Best Ten Films of 1991 by the *Los
Angeles Times*. In 1991 he was awarded the Most
Promising Newcomer to British Film at the *Evening
Standard* Film Awards. His second feature film as both
writer and director, *The Passion of Darkly Noon* (1995),
won the Best Director Award at the Porto Film Festival.
The theme song he co-wrote for this film, 'Who Will
Love Me Now?', was released as a single by P. J. Harvey.
His work has been translated into seventeen languages.

PHILIP RIDLEY

Krindlekrax

faber and faber

First published in 2002
by Faber and Faber Limited
3 Queen Square, London WC1N 3AU

Typeset by Country Setting, Kingsdown, Kent CT14 8ES
Printed in England by Mackays of Chatham plc, Chatham, Kent

A CIP record for this book
is available from the British Library

ISBN 0-571-21543-2

For my grandmother, Cissie –
at the bottom of the stone steps.
I'm calling still.

If the Sun & Moon should Doubt
They'd immediately Go out

William Blake

Krindlekrax was first performed at the Birmingham Repertory Theatre on 20 June 2002. The cast was as follows:

Ruskin Splinter Gregor Henderson-Begg
Wendy Splinter Maria Gough
Winston Splinter Jamie Newall
Corky Pigeon Alan Rothwell
Elvis Cave David Florez
Mr Cave Nick Stringer
Mrs Cave Joy Aldridge
Sparkey Walnut Sushil Chudasama
Dr Flowers John Flitcroft
Mr Lace David Kendall
Mrs Walnut Bharti Patel
Mr Flick Trevor Thomas

Director Anthony Clark
Designer Rachel Blues
Lighting Nick Beadle
Sound Gregory Clarke

Characters

Ruskin Splinter

Wendy Splinter

Winston Splinter

Corky Pigeon

Elvis Cave

Mr Cave

Mrs Cave

Sparkey Walnut

Dr Flowers

Mr Lace

Mrs Walnut

Mr Flick

ACT ONE

Scene One: Dragon Dream
Scene Two: Ruskin's Bedroom
Scene Three: Ruskin's Kitchen
Scene Four: Lizard Street
Scene Five: Classroom
Scene Six: The Playground
Scene Seven: Lizard Street
Scene Eight: Corky's Living Room
Scene Nine: Lizard Street
Scene Ten: Cinema
Scene Eleven: Lizard Street
Scene Twelve: Corky's Living Room
Scene Thirteen: Ruskin's Kitchen
Scene Fourteen: Lizard Street
Scene Fifteen: Ruskin's Bedroom
Scene Sixteen: Lizard Street

ACT TWO

Scene Seventeen: The Sewer
Scene Eighteen: Lizard Street
Scene Nineteen: Ruskin's Bedroom
Scene Twenty: Lizard Street

KRINDLEKRAX

Act One

SCENE ONE: DRAGON DREAM

Darkness.

Silence.

Then –

Dragon (*over speakers, very loud*) RAAAAAHHH!

Slight pause.

RAAAAAHHH!

Ruskin 'Stay back, Dragon!'

Gradually, light comes up on Ruskin. He is eleven years old and wearing striped (green and white) pyjamas and round-rimmed spectacles. He is pale, thin, with frizzy red hair and freckles. In his left hand is a cardboard shield – depicting a green dragon (with red eyes) against a blue sky – and, in his right, a wooden sword (both objects, all too clearly, home-made). He is thrashing his sword at the invisible –

Dragon RAAAAAHHH!

Ruskin 'I am not afraid! I am handsome and strong! Look at my muscles! Listen to my voice – like thunder!'

Dragon RAAAAAHHH!

Ruskin 'I'm warning you, Dragon! This village – it's my home. These villagers – they're my friends. I'm here to protect them. Go back to your cave, Dragon. Don't ever threaten this place again.'

Dragon RAAAAAHHH!

Ruskin 'Take that! And that! And –'

Wendy (*calling, off*) Ruskin!

Ruskin has been backing into (and up onto) a bed.

He is now on his back, in the throes of battle, as –

Wendy (*calling, off*) Ruskin!

Suddenly, Ruskin sits bolt upright as –

SCENE TWO: RUSKIN'S BEDROOM

Morning sunlight abruptly illuminates Ruskin's real surroundings: walls covered with photos of actors, etc., piles of books and, of course, Ruskin gasping –

Ruskin I'm awake, Mum!

Wendy You'll be late for school.

Ruskin Alright, Mum.

Looks at photo.

It's today, fellow thespians – ooo, you don't mind me calling you 'fellow thespians', do you? I know I'll never be as good at acting as you, Sir Laurence Olivier, Sir John Gielgud. Or you, Sir Ralph Richardson. But it's just that today – oh, today I feel so . . . confident. I know the part of hero inside out. Young Hal Oaktree. Farmer boy. I've read books on cattle-breeding and crop rotation. Young Hal Oaktree. Dragon-fighter.

Picks up books.

Mythical creatures. Correct way to hold medieval weapons. Young Hal throws a golden penny. Into Dragon's mouth! Dragon chokes! Thwack! Dragon's head off! Cool, eh? Oh, the school won't know what's hit in when I audition.

4

Sound of a window smashing.

Wendy (*with Winston, screaming, off*) Ahhhhh!

Winston (*with Wendy, screaming, off*) Ahhhhh!

Ruskin Elvis!

SCENE THREE: RUSKIN'S KITCHEN

Sunlight illuminates cooker, fridge, chairs and table.
A football lies in the middle of table and has obviously
smashed much cutlery (including many plates of toast)
and knocked toaster to the floor.

Wendy Splinter is picking up toaster. She is thirty-three
years old and wearing a (faded 'n' frayed) green dressing
gown, fluffy green slippers and round-rimmed spectacles.
She is pale, thin and has frizzy, red hair.

Winston Splinter, her husband, is huddled under the
table, trembling with fear. He is thirty-five years old
and wears striped (green and white) pyjama bottoms,
string vest, green socks and round-rimmed spectacles.
He is pale, thin and balding (what hair remains is frizzy
and red).

Wendy Look at the mess! If the toaster's damaged . . .
well, we can't afford a new one, you know.

Winston Not my fault.

Wendy Someone's got to do something about Elvis.

   Puts bread in toaster.

We'll have no windows left at this rate.

   Ruskin enters, now wearing green shorts, a striped
   (green and white) T-shirt and green, lace-up shoes.
   He is clutching satchel, sword and shield.

5

Ruskin Morning, Mum.

Kisses Wendy.

Wendy Mind where you tread! Elvis is up to his tricks again.

Ruskin So I see. Morning, Dad.

Winston Not my fault.

Ruskin Well . . . today's the day, everyone.

Removes broken crockery from seat and sits.

Wendy Tea?

Pours cup of tea for Ruskin.

Ruskin I've learnt all my lines.

Wendy That's the third window we've lost this month, Winston. I'm still finding glass in the living room. And as for the bathroom . . . well, no privacy there!

Winston Not my fault.

Takes can of lager from fridge.

Ruskin I'm gonna get the part. No problems!

Wendy (*at Winston*) Oi! Bit early for that.

Winston Not my fault.

Wendy No one's forced it down your throat.

Toaster pops.

Aha! One bit of good news.

Ruskin No toast for me, Mum.

Wendy Wh . . . what? No toast! But . . . you always have toast. We all do. Every morning. Kiss! Tea! Toast! . . . You ill?

Ruskin No, no. Just butterflies in belly saying, 'No toast today, young thespian.'

Wendy Thespywhat?

Ruskin *Actor*, Mum. It's the auditions for the school play.

Wendy What school play?

Ruskin *Young Hal Oaktree*. Been telling you about it for weeks.

Wendy Who?

Ruskin You! You! I've shown you the script. Look!

Takes script from satchel.

Lager stains! That's when you looked at it, Dad. And buttery toast from when –

Wendy Toast! You see! Every day.

Ruskin You're not listening! This is only like the most important day in my whole entire life. And all you're worried about is toast and . . . booze!

Wendy (*with Winston*) Ruskin!

Winston (*with Wendy*) Now hang on –

Ruskin I've been learning this speech for ages. Have you asked to hear it? No! Shown any interest at all? No! Am I bothered? Ha! I'm used to it.

Pause.

Wendy Can I . . . can we hear your speech?

Slight pause.

Winston (*with Wendy*) Please.

Wendy (*with Winston*) Please.

Ruskin gets on his chair, holds sword and shield, coughs, takes deep breath and –

Ruskin . . . You ready?

Wendy (*with Winston*) Yes, yes.

Winston (*with Wendy*) Yes, son, yes.

Ruskin 'I am handsome and strong. Look at my muscles.'

Wendy and Winston glance at each other, suppressing giggles.

Ruskin 'Listen to my voice – it's like thunder.'

Wendy and Winston find it more difficult to hide their rising giggles.

Ruskin What? What?

Wendy . . . Nothing.

Winston Forget it.

Laughter takes over.

Ruskin My sword? Is it wonky?

Wendy It's you who's wonky.

Wendy and Winston laugh even louder.

Ruskin Me? What d'you mean . . .? Mum?

Wendy gets her giggles under control and –

Wendy Ruskin . . . are you sure you're auditioning for the . . . right part?

Ruskin Kindly elucidate . . . Explain! Explain!

Wendy Well . . . a line like, 'I am handsome and strong.'

Ruskin What's wrong with it?

Winston You!

Ruskin How?

Wendy You're not strong.

Winston Or handsome.

Ruskin It's acting! Act – ting!

Wendy But . . . what's the next line? Say again.

Ruskin 'Look at my muscles!'

Wendy (*with Winston*) Ha!

Winston (*with Wendy*) Ha!

Ruskin 'Listen to my voice – it's like thunder!'

Wendy It's a squeak.

Winston My belly rumbles louder.

Wendy Honestly, Ruskin, an arthritic mouse with laryngitis has more chance of getting the role of hero than you.

> *Wendy and Winston laugh once more.*
> *Ruskin watches them.*
> *Slight pause.*

Ruskin Well, I'm glad I've supplied you with your morning entertainment.

> *Packs things into satchel.*

Now, if you'll excuse me, my vocation is calling.

> *Turns to leave.*

Wendy Oh, Ruskin, we didn't mean to upset you. Honest.

Winston All we're trying to say is –

9

Ruskin What? Eh?

Wendy Well . . . certain people can play certain parts.

Winston And certain people can't.

Ruskin I do understand the technicalities of casting.

Wendy Then you wouldn't get Charlie Chaplin as James Bond, would you?

Ruskin No. But I wouldn't laugh in his face for trying.

Wendy Oh, Ruskin . . . we're only trying to protect you.

Ruskin From what?

Winston Everyone!

Wendy They'll laugh.

Ruskin Not if I believe it enough.

Wendy Rusk, sweetheart, there's only one person in Lizard Street who could say those lines without causing giggles. You know it. Your Dad knows it. We all know it. Only one person who is handsome enough.

Winston Strong enough.

Wendy Thunder-voiced enough.

Ruskin I . . . I've no idea know who you mean.

Elvis (*calling, off*) I WANT MY BALL!

All Elvis!

SCENE FOUR: LIZARD STREET

The main set – Lizard Street – is now bathed in sunlight. It dominates the stage. On either side: two-storey, red-bricked, terraced houses, including Ruskin's house, a

grocer's, a small (house converted into) cinema called
'Flick's Ritz', a pub – its sign reads, 'The Dragon and
the Golden Penny' – and a house with many flowered
window boxes. Cracks in pavement, a few holes in the
cobbled road, and dark patches on the brickwork. The
street runs down the middle of the stage (like the silent
movie cliché of a path leading to sunset) and should give
the impression of great depth. At the far (sunset) end is
Lizard Street School, St George's, a Victorian monstrosity
with gothic turrets and spiky railings. The set can be as
simple as a painted backdrop, or as elaborate as a fully
built construction.

Lizard Street has, of course, been making its presence
felt from the very beginning but, from now on, becomes
a constant presence. All scenes – including the previous
three – take place in it, singled out by lighting and
minimal props. The impression should be of one scene
effortlessly dissolving into the next.

Elvis Cave stands in street. He is eleven years old and
wearing a black-and-white American footballer outfit
(complete with padded shoulders, tight trousers and
shiny, black helmet with visor). His hair (when visible) is
black and styled in a quiff. He is both tall and muscular
for his age and has a voice that sounds like . . . well,
thunder. Puberty has struck Elvis with the delicacy of
a sledgehammer. Beside him stands Sparkey Walnut. He
is eleven years old and wearing an American baseball
player's outfit (with black cap). His hair (when visible) is
crew cut. He is, like Elvis, tall for his age, but lacks the
rampaging testosterone. Puberty has merely patted him.

Ruskin – who has remained on stage as the scene
changed around him – is already on the street, clutching
sword, shield, satchel and ball, but neither Elvis nor
Sparkey notices him.

Elvis IF YOU DON'T GIMME MY BALL BACK IN FIVE SECONDS THERE'LL BE TROUBLE! I'LL BE IN A BAD MOOD! AND YOU DON'T WANNA SEE ELVIS CAVE IN A BAD MOOD! READY? ONE! TWO! THREE! FOUR! I'M NEARLY AT FIVE NOW! FOUR AND A HALF . . . FOUR AND THREE-QUARTERS! I'M REALLY IN A BAD MOOD NOW! FOUR AND SEVEN-EIGHTHS –

Ruskin Boo!

Elvis jumps, startled.

Elvis Ahh! Don't creep up like that.

Ruskin and Sparkey playfully smile at each other. Both amused by Ruskin's 'Boo!'

Ruskin Morning, Sparkey.

Sparkey Morning, Rusk.

Ruskin Morning, Elvis.

Elvis Ball! Now!

Ruskin gives ball to Elvis.

Elvis Ugh . . . it's sticky.

Ruskin Marmalade.

Elvis Couldn't you clean it?

Ruskin Not in five seconds, no.

Elvis points at Ruskin's wooden sword.

Elvis Ha! What's that supposed to be?

Ruskin My sword. Made it myself.

Elvis Don't tell me! Oh, no! It can't be! Sparkey! He's gonna audition for the hero . . . Ha! Ha! Ha! – Laugh! Laugh!

Sparkey Ha! Ha!

Elvis and Sparkey continue laughing.
Ruskin watches, impassive.
Slight pause.

Ruskin Go on. Say it. 'You ain't got any muscles.'

Elvis I've got bogies with more muscles.

Ruskin Bogies can't act. I can.

Elvis Act like a poop stick, you mean.

Ruskin Act like Sir Laurence Olivier. Sir John Gielgud.
Sir Ralph Rich –

Elvis Who? Who?

Ruskin Famous actors.

Elvis Well, I ain't seen 'em in anything.

Ruskin They ain't been in anything for a while.

Elvis Trust you to like has-beens.

Ruskin They're not has-beens they're . . . dead.

Elvis (*with Sparkey*) Dead!

Sparkey (*with Elvis*) Dead!

Ruskin So?

Elvis So . . . you've been taught by a bunch of stiffs.
They're history! His – storr – ree! Ain't got nothing to
teach no one! Except how to rot. No wonder your acting
stinks. Ha!

Sparkey Ha!

Elvis Now me – I've been taught by actors live and
kicking.

Ruskin Taught by –? You re going to audition?

Elvis Part's mine for the asking.

Ruskin Know the lines?

Elvis What's that got to do with it?

Ruskin Philistine.

Elvis Thanks.

Ruskin It's an insult.

*Elvis grabs Ruskin round the neck.
    Ruskin struggles, dropping sword, etc.*

Elvis Looks like you need some manners scratched into
your head.

Starts scratching Ruskin's head.

Ruskin Ouch! Stop it, Elvis!

Elvis Don't make a fuss.

*Dr Flowers comes out of his house. He is fifty years
old and wearing a grey tweed suit. His hair is thinning
and greying and he's clutching a green medical bag.
He notices Ruskin's plight, but tries his best to ignore
it, sniffing the flowers in his window boxes. Finally,
though, Ruskin's cries get to him and –*

Dr Flowers Elvis! Sparkey!

Elvis (*with Sparkey*) Morning, Doc.

Sparkey (*with Elvis*) Morning, Doc.

Dr Flowers Stop tormenting poor Ruskin! Now, Elvis!
NOW!

*Elvis gasps, jolted by the volume of Dr Flowers' last
'NOW!' He lets go of Ruskin and, for a moment,
looks totally fazed.*

Elvis Everyone . . . everyone's always picking on me!
Just 'cos I'm big for my age. Can't help being tall. Can't
help having muscles.

Dr Flowers Elvis, all I'm saying is –

Elvis Come on, Sparkey. Let's go. Before I get blamed for something else.

Elvis and Sparkey walk down the street and exit.

Dr Flowers You alright, Ruskin?

Ruskin Yeah. Used to it.

Wendy comes out of house, holding large plate of uneaten toast.
She chucks toast down drain, then –

Wendy Oh! Morning, Doctor Flow – Ruskin! What happened?

Dr Flowers It was Elvis. Scratching Ruskin's head again.

Wendy Why didn't you call out for me? I feel terrible now.

Ruskin It's not your fault, Mum.

Dr Flowers Elvis's bullying isn't anyone's fault. It's just . . . Elvis. He's turning into such a . . . nightmare.

Ruskin No! Don't say that! Elvis is . . . He might be doing some nightmare things but . . . well, *he's* not a nightmare.

Dr Flowers Ruskin, how can you say that after he –?

Ruskin He's a neighbour! A Lizard Street neighbour. And Lizard Street is supposed to be the most friendly street in the whole world. Right?

Dr Flowers Supposed to be, yes.

Ruskin It is! No buts! We've gotta have faith in Lizard Street. You know the Lizard Street Anthem.

Singing to the tune Parry put to William Blake's 'Jerusalem'.

15

Ruskin
'And did that hero Hal Oaktree
Battle a Dragon –?'

Come on! Join in!

Wendy Oh, Ruskin, you know I don't like to sing any more.

Ruskin Try, Mum! Try!

Dubiously, Wendy and Dr Flowers join in.
Wendy's voice is tremulous, barely audible.

All
'And did that hero, Hal Oaktree,
Battle a Dragon where we stand?
And did the hero change the scene
Into this pleasant land serene?'

The school bell rings.
They all stop singing and –

All School!

SCENE FIVE: CLASSROOM

Mr Lace stands in front of class. He is fifty years old, with thinning hair, and wearing a (somewhat frayed) tweed jacket (with a flower in the lapel), shoes (well worn) and a green scarf (quite threadbare). In fact, everything about him – including nerves – is threadbare.

Ruskin, Elvis and Sparkey sit at desks.

Mr Lace Friends, fellow thespians, youth of Lizard Street, lend me your ears.

Ruskin is attentive.
Elvis and Sparkey mutter and giggle.

Mr Lace At last! Our journey to St George's School production of *Young Hal Oaktree* starts here. Oh, that masterpiece of a play! Young Hal helps a Wizard. The Wizard gives him a golden penny – oh, the symbolism! Later, when Young Hal's village is threatened by a Dragon, he –

Ruskin Throws the penny!

Mr Lace Into the Dragon's mouth!

Ruskin The Dragon chokes!

Mr Lace And in that instant –

Ruskin Chop!

Mr Lace Off with the Dragon's head! Oh, what a legend! What poetry! Ever since I first found the original manuscript I've been dreaming of presenting the play to the people of Lizard Street – Elvis? Are you listening?

Elvis Er . . . nah!

Mr Lace Oh, Elvis! What's happened to you? You used to be so proud of our legend. Didn't you? Look at me, Elvis. And you should be proud that we are the only street in the whole country to have a play written about it by . . . well, written by the one and only Bard whose name sends me into paroxysms of delight.

Elvis No proof!

Mr Lace Of what?

Elvis Who wrote the play! It's just a rumour. Started by you!

Ruskin Mr Lace found the manuscript in his back garden. In a special box marked, 'MY FAVOURITE PLAY – EVEN BETTER THAN HAMLET.'

Elvis My Dad says you put it there.

Mr Lace Me?

Ruskin Mr Lace found writing on his garden wall too. 'I LODGED HERE FOR A WHILE. SIGNED WILLIAM SHAKESP –'

Mr Lace Don't say it, Ruskin!

Elvis Dad says you wrote that too.

Mr Lace Slander! I would never slur the name of Shakes –

Ruskin Don't say it, Mr Lace!

Elvis Dad says you didn't even write the play properly.

Mr Lace The spelling was faultless.

Ruskin It was! I've seen it!

Elvis It's in felt-tip pen. Didn't have felt-tip pen in the time of Shakes –

Ruskin (*with Mr Lace*) Don't say it, Elvis!

Mr Lace (*with Ruskin*) Don't say it, Elvis.

Elvis Can say what I like! . . . Shakespeare!

Mr Lace That name! The Maestro of Magic! The DNA of all theatre!

   Clutches chest, legs wobbling.

Elvis Shakespeare! – Come on, Sparkey!

Sparkey (*with Elvis*) Shakespeare!

Elvis (*with Sparkey*) Shakespeare!

Mr Lace Ahhh! My skin tingles! 'Those are pearls that were his –' Oh, the alchemy! 'Fear no more the heat o' the sun . . .' We are not worthy! None of us are!

Elvis (*with Sparkey*) Shakespeare!

Sparkey (*with Elvis*) Shakespeare!

Mr Lace Ahhh, no, no. Please!

Falls to his knees.

Ruskin Stop Shakespearing, Mr Lace!

Mr Lace cries out at Ruskin's 'Shakespearing'.

Ruskin Sorry, Mr Lace!

Elvis Shakespeare! Why should I?

Mr Lace Ahhh, no, no! 'That father lost, lost his . . .'

Ruskin If you don't stop Shakespearing, Mr Lace – oh, sorry, Mr Lace – we'll never –

Elvis (*with Sparkey*) Shakespeare!

Sparkey (*with Elvis*) Shakespeare!

Ruskin – we'll *never* have the auditions and Mr Lace will never be able to choose the hero.

Slight pause.

Elvis . . . Alright, alright.

Ruskin rushes to Mr Lace.

Ruskin Mr Lace! Where's your smelling salts?

Mr Lace indicates his desk drawer.
    Ruskin gets smelling salts and holds them under
Mr Lace's nose.

Ruskin Think of everyday life.

Mr Lace Every . . . day . . . life . . . What's that?

Ruskin Cutting your toenails. Brushing your teeth. No milk for your tea.

Mr Lace No milk!

Ruskin That's it, Mr Lace! Come on! No hot water for your bath . . . Running out of toilet paper . . . That's it! That's it!

Slowly, Mr Lace is getting back to his feet.

Mr Lace Thank you, Ruskin. Remind me to pop into Mrs Walnut's for a pint of milk after school. Yes! I'm . . . poetically de-toxed . . . Now, we . . . we were about to do the auditions. Am I right?

Ruskin You are, Mr Lace.

Mr Lace So . . . who's first?

Elvis Me!

Elvis stands in front of class, clutching his sports bag.

Mr Lace Now . . . imagine where you are, Elvis. On a lonely hillside. The Dragon is in front of you. It's threatening the village. You are about to fight it. Begin when you've found your motivation and –

Elvis has taken large, plastic weapons from his sports bag: space guns, water-shooting bazookas. They make noises as he fires and –

Elvis Die, Dragon! I'm the hero! I'M THE HERO!!

Elvis glares at Mr Lace,
*   then looks at Ruskin and grins.*
*   Ruskin looks from Elvis to Mr Lace.*
*   Mr Lace looks at Ruskin.*

Ruskin NOOOOOOO!!!

Classroom dissolves away as Ruskin screams (Elvis, Mr Lace and Sparkey rushing off with desks, etc.) and the scene becomes –

SCENE SIX: PLAYGROUND

– where Ruskin's scream turns to whimpering.

Ruskin It's not . . . fair! It just not fair!

Corky appears, sweeping. He is sixty-five years old, white-haired (and moustached), and is wearing a white protective work coat and spectacles. He walks with a slight limp.

Corky Ruskin?

Ruskin Oh, Corky!

Ruskin rushes into Corky's arms and bursts into tears.

Corky Oh, my dear boy, what happened?

Ruskin Learning lines . . . Shield . . . Sword . . . Hero . . . Me . . . You know?

Corky Of course, dear boy.

Ruskin Today . . . Elvis . . . says he's gonna . . . Him! Big voice! Boom! Class cheers and claps. Mr Lace whispers in my ear, 'Perhaps it's best if you don't audition, Ruskin.'

Corky What! Why, I might just be the school caretaker, but I'll give him what-for. He needs his head examined.

Ruskin It's me who needs his head examined.

Corky And why's that?

Ruskin Oh, Corky. Me? A hero? Even Mum and Dad laughed.

Corky What if they did? Why, the way you learnt that speech. Such love for language. Look at me, my boy. Look! Laugh, indeed. You're in good company. Everyone laughed at Turner – you know him? A painter. Years ago – They laughed when they saw his paintings. Everyone thought his glorious sunsets were nothing but dirty dishcloths. But you know what? Everyone was wrong! And don't forget William Blake. One of the greatest visionaries who ever lived. People laughed at him too. But did it put old Bill Blake off? Not one jot! You know what he said? 'If the sun and moon should doubt, they'd immediately go out.' And that's you, my boy. You're the sun and moon. And I won't let you start doubting yourself because of a few laughing . . . sillybillies. You hear me?

Ruskin . . . Yes, Corky.

Corky Now, pick up your shield and sword. I feel a pot of tea and chocky-bickies coming on.

Corky discards his broom, picks up his walking stick, and they step into –

SCENE SEVEN: LIZARD STREET

The street is bursting with activity. Mr and Mrs Cave are hanging a home-made banner (it reads, 'ELVIS CAVE IS THE HERO IN THE SCHOOL PLAY') outside pub. They are both overweight and smoking cigars. Mr Cave – who is almost totally bald – is wearing a black tracksuit. Mrs Cave is wearing a black tracksuit and too much hair and make-up.

Mrs Cave (*with Mr Cave*) Corky!

Mr Cave (*with Mrs Cave*) Corky!

Mrs Cave Have you heard?

Mr Cave My son.

Mrs Cave *Our* son.

Mr Cave (*with Mrs Cave*) The hero!

Mrs Cave (*with Mr Cave*) The hero!

Corky Oh, yes, I . . . I did hear something.

Mrs Cave What d'ya think of the banner?

Mr Cave Made it myself.

Mrs Cave *We* made it.

Mr Cave Made these too . . .

Hands a flyer to Corky.

Corky (*reading*) 'The Theatrical Event of the Millennium.'

Mr Cave It will be.

Corky 'Elvis Cave will give the greatest performance ever witnessed when he plays the hero in the school play! See him and cheer! Or else.' Mmm, very . . . persuasive.

Mrs Cave Oh, my little Elvy-baby. He'll have his name in lights one day.

Mr Cave Everything he touches will be a smash.

Ruskin Like our windows.

Mrs Cave No jealousy, please.

Ruskin Jealousy!

Mrs Cave Oh, Ruskin, Elvis told us you wanted to play the part. But . . .

Mr Cave The better man won.

Ruskin The loudest, you mean.

Mr Cave Loudness is all that matters, ol' son! Ain't that school taught you nothing?

Corky Now, now, now, let's not get tetchy with each other. I'm sure Elvis will try his best to give a performance of great . . .

Ruskin Volume?

Corky Energy.

Mr Cave Oh, he'll have energy alright. Takes after his old man. More energy than a truckload of batteries, me. Eh, Mrs Cave?

Mrs Cave Ooo, I'd say.

Mr Cave has spied Dr Flowers strolling down the street. Mr Cave and Mrs Cave rush to him, waving flyers in the air.

Mr Cave (*with Mrs Cave*) Dr Flowers!

Mrs Cave (*with Mr Cave*) Dr Flowers!

We catch a little of their 'Have you heard? Our son?' etc. routine.

Corky Don't let it bother you, my boy. Art is like champagne. Only the bubbles rise quickly.

Ruskin Mmm . . .

Slight pause.

Corky Well, would you look at that!

Points at cobbles.

Most interesting. See, my boy? Look!

Ruskin . . . What?

Corky A hole! Here! There's more and more lately.

Slight pause.

Its claws must be getting very long.

Ruskin Claws?

Corky Wh . . . what? Oh, nothing. Forget it, my boy. Come on! I'm dying for that cup of tea.

Ruskin No, Corky! You said *claws*. What claws –?

Mr Flick Afternoon, Corky.

Mr Flick has appeared. He is in his late fifties and wearing a black suit with velvet lapels, black bow tie, velvet, emerald-green waistcoat (with brass buttons) and shiny patent-leather shoes. He is carrying cans of film.

Corky Afternoon, Mr Flick. New film?

Mr Flick Indeed it is. *Henry V*. Starring Sir Laurence Olivier.

Corky You hear that, my boy?

Mr Flick Thought it might inspire you, Ruskin.

Ruskin Don't bother!

Mr Flick Don't both –? What on earth do you mean?

Corky Haven't you seen . . .?

Indicates banner.

Mr Flick Impossible!

Ruskin Possible!

Mr Flick But . . . how?

Corky I'm afraid Mr Lace has succumbed to the –

Ruskin Yob culture!

Mr Flick Oh, Ruskin. I'm sorry. What a loss not seeing your performance will be. But . . . well, you mustn't let it get you down. Come and see the film anyway. Free tickets. How's that?

Corky Very kind, Mr Flick, I'm sure Ruskin will enjoy –

Mr Cave (*with Mrs Cave*) Mr Flick!

Mrs Cave (*with Mr Cave*) Mr Flick!

Mr Cave and Mrs Cave have spied Mr Flick and are rushing over, waving flyers in the air (and launching into their 'Have you heard?' etc. routine).

Corky 'Bye, Mr Flick.

Mr Flick 'Bye, Corky. 'Bye, Ruskin.

Ruskin and Corky move away.

Corky Don't let it –

Ruskin Bother me. I know, I know.

Slight pause.

Corky Look!

Points at pavement.

A crack! See it, my boy? There's been more and more lately.

Slight pause.

Its tail must be getting very heavy.

Ruskin Tail?

Corky Wh . . . what? Oh, nothing. Forget it, my boy. Come on! Let's get some chockie-bickies to go with that tea.

Ruskin No, Corky! You said tail! What tail –?

Corky Afternoon, Mrs Walnut.

Mrs Walnut, Sparkey's mum, has come out of her grocer's shop. She is forty-two years old, thin, and wearing a green apron. She holds a packet of biscuits.

Mrs Walnut Corky! And how are you today?

Corky In need of a packet of your best chocky-bickies, if you please, Mrs Walnut.

Mrs Walnut Voilà!

Hands him biscuits.

Corky Am I that predictable?

Mrs Walnut Nothing wrong with that.

Corky Anything else you want, my boy?

Ruskin shakes his head and murmurs in the negative.

Mrs Walnut Ooo, why the long face, Ruskin?

Corky indicates Mr and Mrs Cave.

Mrs Walnut Oh! That! I saw them preparing it all this morning.

Ruskin This morning! We didn't have the auditions until this afternoon.

Mrs Walnut I guess they just . . . knew.

Ruskin 'Course they knew! Everyone knew! Whatever Elvis wants, Elvis gets!

Mrs Walnut Oh, how did it all get like this? You and Sparkey and Elvis were all best friends once. The three of you went everywhere together. You used to sit in Sparkey's room for hours and hours. Laughing and chatting and – oh, the memory of it!

Corky It'll be like that again, Mrs Walnut.

Mrs Walnut But when, Corky? That's what I want to know. And how? With Elvis bouncing that ball all over the place and breaking windows. I've had to replace my shop front three times. Can't afford that. It's just me, you know. I've got no Mr Walnut to help.

Mr Cave (*with Mrs Cave*) Mrs Walnut!

Mrs Cave (*with Mr Cave*) Mrs Walnut!

Mr Cave and Mrs Cave have spied Mrs Walnut and rush over, waving flyers.

Corky 'Bye, Mrs Walnut.

Mrs Walnut 'Bye, Corky. 'Bye, Ruskin.

Once more, we catch Mr Cave and Mrs Cave doing their 'Have you heard' etc. routine as Corky and Ruskin walk away . . .

Ruskin Don't say it. 'Don't let it bother you. Only bubbles.'

Corky Look!

Points at wall.

Another burnt patch. See it, my boy? There's been more and more lately. Mmm . . .

Slight pause.

Its breath must be getting very hot.

Ruskin Breath?

Corky Wh . . . what? Oh, nothing! Forget it, my boy.

Ruskin No, Corky! You said breath! *Hot* breath! Whose hot –?

Wendy (*with Winston*) Hello, Corky!

Winston (*with Wendy*) Hello, Corky!

Winston and Wendy have appeared, each carrying a pane of glass.

Corky Good afternoon, Wendy. Good afternoon, Winston.

Wendy We've bought some new glass.

Corky Expensive, eh?

Wendy Can't stand the drafts any more.

Winston Not my fault.

Corky Ruskin's coming to my place for a cuppa, if that's alright. He needs a bit of cheering up.

Wendy Cheering up . . . ?

Notices commotion in the street.

Oh. Well . . . I warned you. Didn't I?

Winston Didn't *we*?

Ruskin Alright, alright.

Mrs Cave Oi! You two!

Mrs Cave rushes over to Wendy and Winston, waving flyers.

Ruskin Oh, let's go, Corky. Please.

Elvis THE HERO IS HERE!

Elvis appears, brandishing space guns, etc. Sparkey is at his side.

Mr Lace follows.

Mr Cave and Mrs Cave rush over to Elvis and start cheering. Everyone else, except Ruskin and Corky, feels compelled to follow suit.

Mr Cave and Mrs Cave lift Elvis – not as easily as they had hoped – onto their shoulders. They begin a chant of 'Hero! Hero!' The others, once more, feel compelled to join in.

Ruskin Come on! Quick!

Corky Not like this.

Ruskin Like what?

Corky With that look in your eyes. Like you . . . like you don't love Lizard Street any more.

Ruskin How can I? Listen!

Corky I know it's difficult. But you've got to rise above it. This is Lizard Street. The Friendliest Street in the Whole World.

Ruskin I know that, Corky, but look at –

Corky Then say it! Tell the street you love it! If you don't, you've let the bullies win. Prove how strong you really are, my boy. Go on.

Slight pause.

Do it for me.

Slowly, Ruskin takes a deep breath and –

Ruskin I LOVE YOU, LIZARD STREET!

Everyone stares at Ruskin in stunned silence.
  Slight pause.
  Then –

A whistling kettle transforms the scene into –

SCENE EIGHT: CORKY'S LIVING ROOM

The room is suggested by armchair, cooker, sideboard, and some framed photos.

Corky pours hot water from kettle into teapot, then brings pot to chair. He sits and smiles at Ruskin, who is cross-legged on the floor.

Ruskin So . . . tell me!

Corky Tell you what, my boy?

Ruskin You know! What caused the holes? And cracks. And burnt bits of wall.

Corky Told you. Its claws. Its tail. Its breath.

Ruskin But what is . . . *it*?

Corky Oh . . . that's my secret.

Ruskin You can tell me. I'm your friend, ain't I?

Corky My very best.

Ruskin And you're my very best, too. Ain't you, Corky?

Corky For ever and always.

Ruskin And for ever and always friends shouldn't have secrets.

Slight pause.

Well, should they?

Corky Loòk in that top drawer, my boy. Go on!

Ruskin goes to drawer and removes a steel helmet with torch on.

Ruskin What is it?

Corky I used to wear it.

Ruskin For what?

Corky The job I had. Before I was a caretaker.

Ruskin Before you were a caretaker?

Corky Well, I wasn't born a caretaker, you know. And I wasn't born with white hair and a face full of wrinkles either. I know it may come as a bit of a shock, my boy, but once . . . I was young.

Ruskin Can't imagine you young.

Corky Can't imagine it myself any more. But young I was. A young sewer inspector.

Ruskin Sewer inspector!

Corky My job. I'd put that thing on and – Here!

Puts helmet on.

I'd climb down ladder into the darkness and –

Turns torch on, looks round.

Oooo!

Ruskin What the sewers look like, Corky?

Corky Like . . . big tube-train tunnels. Except there's water instead of railway lines. Of course, when I say water I mean . . . sludge! Smelly green sludge thick as . . . well, the thickest snot you've ever sneezed.

Ruskin Yeah! I . . . I see it.

Corky And the walls! You see them? Covered with slime.

Ruskin Yeah.

Corky And the smell! Ugh!

Ruskin Ugh! Like sour milk.

Corky Oh, worse than that.

Ruskin Dad's socks.

Corky Worse.

Ruskin . . . A million Dad's socks!

Corky Exactly, my boy. A million Dad's socks.

Gasps.

Ruskin What?

Corky A rat!

Ruskin Where?

Corky There!

Ruskin Ahhh!

Corky And there! There! Hundreds of them! Listen to them squealing. Swimming in the slime and scrambling along the pathways. Don't worry, my boy. They'll pass in a minute . . . That's it . . .

Ruskin They're going?

Corky Yes . . . It should be easier along here. The water's not too deep. Check for cracks in the wall, will you?

Ruskin Is that what you do, Corky?

Corky It is. I check for damage. Any damage at all –

Gasps.

Ruskin What?

Corky A . . . strange sound.

Ruskin Like what?

Corky Like . . . an animal cry!

Ruskin A rat?

Corky No, no . . . There it is again! Oh, I've never heard anything like it before. A terrible, vicious rasping sound –

Gasps.

Ruskin What now?

Corky Splashing! Something's moving in the water.

Ruskin What is it?

Corky It's getting closer –

Gasps.

Ruskin What? What?

Corky Look! It's green! The size of a . . . a skateboard! It's getting closer and closer – Red eyes! Teeth! Sharp teeth! Like razors!

Ruskin Run!

Corky I am! Ahhh!

Ruskin What?

Corky It's chasing after me!

Ruskin Faster!

Corky It's catching up! Splashing! Snarling! Aha! The ladder!

Ruskin Climb it!

Corky Up! Up! Ahhh!

Ruskin What?

Corky It's biting my knee. Ahhhh!

Ruskin Kick it off!

Corky I'm trying. Ahhh! Its teeth are digging deeper and deeper – There! It's gone! I hear it splash into the sludge below . . . I'm on the street now. Phew!

Flops into armchair.

Ruskin What . . . what *was* it, Corky?

Corky Can't be sure, my boy. But it appeared to be . . . oh, surely not.

Ruskin What, what?

Corky A baby crocodile.

Ruskin But . . . how'd it get down there?

Corky No idea. Oh, just thinking about it makes my blood run cold.

Ruskin You're safe now, Corky. With me. Safe and sound.

Corky Safe, my boy. But not altogether sound.

Touches leg.

Ruskin Your limp!

Corky Had to stop going down the sewers after that. My leg couldn't cope with all those slippery ladders. They gave me a job in the office. Very kind of them, of course.

Removes helmet.

But . . . oh, how I miss those sewers . . . Another biscuit, my dear boy?

Ruskin Thanks.

Takes biscuit.

Corky And then, one day, a stroke of luck. Flu had laid off all the sewer inspectors. And there was a leak. A bad one. Someone had to get down there urgently. But who? Who could go? Mmm?

Ruskin Corky to the rescue!

Corky puts helmet back on.

Corky My limp made things difficult but . . . oh, I didn't mind. I was back! Back in my sewer! My glorious sewer! Now where's the damage . . . ?

Looks round.

Ruskin Found it yet?

Corky No. I'm moving deeper and deeper into the sewer now. This is . . . oh, this is the abandoned section. Unused for years. Never been this far before . . . Look!

Ruskin What?

Corky A huge chamber. Big as a cathedral! Walls like rock . . . like a cave. Yes, a vast cave. Oh, it's so beautiful. The slime glistens like emeralds.

Gasps.

Ruskin What?

Corky I . . . I can hear breathing. The loudest, deepest breathing I've ever – It's getting closer . . . The water's moving all around me . . . Like the tide coming in . . . Whatever it is – oh, it's huge! Ahhhh!!

Puts hands over ears.

Ruskin What, Corky? What?

Corky A roar! The most deafening roar! It's the crocodile! It's grown! Grown into . . . oh, I don't want to see!

Ruskin Run!

Corky You bet I run! Noooo!

Ruskin What?

Corky It's after me! I can see its shadow on the wall. Oh, it's gigantic. As wide as the sewer itself. And – oh, look. Glimpses of claws! Teeth! Like carving knives!

Ruskin Get out!

Corky Hot breath on my back!

Ruskin Go! Go!

Corky It's going to kill me! I know it! I'm going to dieeeee . . .

Collapses on seat.

Ruskin But . . . you didn't die, did you, Corky?

Corky No, my boy. I didn't die. But later, when I looked in the mirror, I see . . . my hair is white. The monster has drained all the colour from me.

Ruskin Did you tell anyone, Corky?

Corky No one would believe me.

Ruskin But you saw it! Your knee! Hair!

Corky 'Hallucination!' That's what everyone said. I panicked in the dark, slipped and fell – that's how I got my knee – and hallucinated the whole thing.

Ruskin But you didn't.

Corky I know that. You know that. But other people . . . Hallucinations can happen in the sewers, you see. The smelly sock stink gets in your head and you see all sorts. Why, I even saw Queen Victoria down there once. Never met such a misery-guts.

Ruskin But the giant crocodile . . . it wasn't a hallucination, was it?

Corky No, my boy. It wasn't. And it was much more than just a giant crocodile.

Ruskin What d'you mean?

Corky It was . . . Krindlekrax.

Ruskin Krindlekrax?

Corky A legendary creature. Part crocodile, part dragon. A creature that emerges at night when everyone sleeps. And makes holes in the road.

Ruskin And cracks on the pavement.

Corky And burns brickwork.

Ruskin Wow!

Corky You like that, eh?

Wendy (*calling, off*) Ruskin!

Ruskin Teatime.

Corky You best go, my boy.

Ruskin See you tomorrow, Corky.

Corky Of course. Always and for ever.

Ruskin Always and for ever.

> *Ruskin and Corky embrace, then Ruskin walks into –*

SCENE NINE: LIZARD STREET

The sun is setting now. Everything tinged with orange.

Slowly, Ruskin approaches the large drain cover in front of his house.

Ruskin It's down there.

> *Kneels.*

Hello . . .? Hello . . .?

> *Sparkey appears.*
> *He watches Ruskin.*
> *Slight pause.*

Sparkey Hiya.

> *Ruskin yelps and jumps to his feet.*
> *Sparkey yelps at Ruskin's scream.*
> *Slight pause.*

Sparkey What . . . what ya doing?

Ruskin Oh . . . I lost something.

Sparkey Valuable?

Ruskin Nah.

Slight pause.

Sparkey (*with Ruskin*) I'm sorry you didn't get the part –

Ruskin (*with Sparkey*) Had a chat with your mum earlier and –

Sparkey Sorry.

Ruskin Sorry.

Slight pause.

Sparkey (*with Ruskin*) You're a better actor and –

Ruskin (*with Sparkey*) Your mum knew Corky wanted biscuits –

Sparkey Sorry.

Ruskin Sorry.

Slight pause.

Sparkey takes photo from pocket and gives it to Ruskin.

Ruskin What's this?

Sparkey Cut it out of a magazine. Photo of that actor you like . . . Albert Heineken!

Ruskin Alec Guinness.

Sparkey Had it on me for ages. Been trying to give it to you but . . . you know.

Ruskin Yeah.

Sparkey Not torn or anything, is it?

Ruskin Nah. It's . . . perfect.

Wendy (*calling, off*) Ruskin!

Ruskin Coming, Mum!

Sparkey Your mum still cook her apple crumble?

Ruskin Yeah.

Sparkey Used to love that. Remember when she got her tongue in a twist and said, 'Fancy a slice of crapple umble?'

Ruskin We burst out laughing.

Sparkey Couldn't stop.

Ruskin Custard came out your nose.

Sparkey Bit of apple came out of yours.

Ruskin Nah! Crapple umble!

   They laugh even more.

Elvis (*calling, off*) Sparkey!

   The laughing stops.

Sparkey I've been buying batteries for his Super Ray Gun Alien Blaster.

   Slight pause.

It should've been you, Rusk. That's all I wanna say.

Elvis (*calling, off*) Sparkey!

Wendy (*calling, off*) Ruskin!

   Ruskin and Sparkey look at each other for a beat longer.
    Then –

They both rush off in different directions.

Fade to black.
    Then –

SCENE TEN: CINEMA

Actor (*over speakers*) 'Once more unto the breach, dear friends, once more . . .'

A cinema projector flickers into life.
    Its light shines out of darkness at the audience, as if the screen is at the back of the auditorium. Cinema seats are lined up in front of projector, facing audience.

Ruskin sits in one of these seats, avidly watching screen.

The film is Henry V *and, although we can't see it, we can certainly hear it. (This can either be the actual soundtrack of Laurence Olivier's film, or a replica. Either way, some careful sound editing is required in order not only to get the battle following the speech but to synchronise the whole thing to what's happening on the stage). The soundtrack has continued without break since opening the scene in darkness . . .*

Actor (*over speakers*)
    '. . . Or close the wall up with our English dead!
In peace there's nothing so becomes a man
As modest stillness and humility:
But when the blast of war blows in our ears . . .'
(*Etc., etc.*)

Corky enters, holding two tubs of popcorn.
    He gives one to Ruskin, then sits.

Ruskin whispers in Corky's ear, bringing him up to speed with the film.

Corky nods enthusiastically.
They watch the film and eat popcorn.
Slight pause.

Mr Flick enters with a torch.
Behind him is Dr Flowers, clutching popcorn.
Mr Flick helps Dr Flowers to seat.
Dr Flowers nods and thanks Mr Flick.
Mr Flick exits.

Dr Flowers sees Corky and Ruskin.
They all exchange waves and smiles.
All three enjoy the film, munching popcorn.
Slight pause.

Mr Flick enters with torch.
Behind him is Mr Lace clutching popcorn.
Mr Flick helps Mr Lace to seat.
Mr Lace nods and thanks Mr Flick.
Mr Flick exits.

Mr Lace sees Corky, Ruskin and Dr Flowers.
They all exchange waves and smiles.
All four enjoy the film, munching popcorn.
Slight pause.

Mr Flick enters with torch.
Behind him is Mrs Walnut, clutching popcorn.
Mr Flick helps Mrs Walnut to a seat.
Mrs Walnut nods and thanks Mr Flick.
Mr Flick exits.

Mrs Walnut sees Corky, Ruskin, Dr Flowers and Mr Lace.
They all exchange waves and smiles.
All five enjoy the film, munching popcorn.
Slight pause.

Ruskin cheers out loud at something on the screen.
Corky motions for him to be quiet.
Ruskin nods.

*The soundtrack to the film is now the beginning of
a horse charge:*
  Hooves thumping, battle cries, music building, etc.
  As this starts –

Elvis bursts in with Sparkey.
  Both are clutching popcorn.
  Mr Flick rushes after them with torch.
  Elvis snatches torch from Mr Flick.
  Mr Flick yelps in shock.

Ruskin Shhh!

*Dr Flowers, Mr Lace and Mrs Walnut glance at
commotion.*
  Corky indicates Ruskin should try to ignore it.
  Ruskin stares at screen as –

*Elvis and Sparkey, as noisily as possible, make their
way to seats.*
  *They are giggling, stumbling, throwing popcorn at
each other, etc.*

Ruskin Shhhh!

Again, Corky indicates Ruskin should ignore them.
  Again, Ruskin tries to concentrate on film.
  Slight pause.

Elvis starts throwing popcorn at Ruskin.
  Ruskin tried to ignore it.
  Finally he snaps and with an angry cry –

Ruskin jumps to his feet.
  Elvis jumps to his feet.
  Corky pulls Ruskin back down.

Elvis bursts out laughing.
  Sparkey joins in.
  Slight pause.

Elvis starts bouncing ball.
  Slight pause.

Mr Lace jumps to his feet and –

Mr Lace Shhhh!

Elvis jumps to his feet.
  Mr Lace and Elvis glare at each other.
  Eventually, Mr Lace sits.

Elvis sits and laughs.
  Sparkey laughs.
  Slight pause.

*The soundtrack of the projected film echoes the rising
tension in the auditorium: battling soldiers, yells,
screams, clanking armour – everything synchronised
to the unfolding drama in the cinema.*

Elvis throws his ball at Dr Flowers' head.
  Dr Flowers yells out.

Mrs Walnut and Mr Lace jump to their feet and –

Mrs Walnut Shhhh!

Mr Lace Shhhh!

Ruskin picks Elvis's ball up.
  Elvis reaches out for it.
  Ruskin won't give it back.

Elvis tugs at the ball.
  Ruskin holds on tighter.

*Mr Lace, Dr Flowers, Mrs Walnut and Corky try to
calm Elvis.*

Elvis grabs Ruskin and starts scratching his head.
  Ruskin yells out.

Mr Flick rushes in.

*There's general pandemonium now: Ruskin screaming,
Elvis laughing, Sparkey giggling, others crying out in
protest and distress. Then just as it seems it can't get
any worse –*

Elvis Shakespeare!

*Mr Lace squeals and falls to his knees.
   Mr Flick is pushed to the floor.
   Ruskin struggles free and pushes Elvis.
   Elvis, caught off balance, stumbles over. He jumps
right back up, grabs ball and, with a roar of anger,
goes to kick the ball. As he does so –*

*Darkness.
   The sound of something tearing!
   Then (and still in darkness) –*

Mr Flick Oh, my screen! My beautiful screen!

SCENE ELEVEN: LIZARD STREET

*Lights come up on Ruskin, Corky, Dr Flowers, Mr Lace
and Mrs Walnut, all clustered round – and comforting –
a distraught Mr Flick.*

Mr Flick Elvis – he did it on purpose! You all saw that!
He aimed the ball. Kicked. Right through the middle of
my . . . my . . . oh, I can't bear to think about it! That
screen has been with me since the very beginning. Every
film has flickered on its smooth, pristine . . . oh! Oh!

Dr Flowers I'll give you some anti-depressant tablets.

Mrs Walnut We need some anti-Elvis tablets.

Corky Oh, I'm sure Elvis can't be all that bad.

Mr Flick Can't be all that –? Honestly, Corky, you and
me have been friends since I don't know when, but I'm

not having you defend that boy. It's not just a cinema screen he's ripped in half. It's my heart. My life. Oh, when I think of how it used to be . . .

Corky Exactly. And Elvis is still that same little boy who used to laugh and play games. You know, I found him sleepwalking down the street a few nights ago and he looked so . . . lost.

Mrs Walnut Sleepwalking?

Dr Flowers Oh, yes, he's started sleepwalking.

Mr Lace And sleep-smashing. He broke one of my windows while he was happily dozing.

Corky Oh, he didn't look happy to me. Not a bit. I'd never seen such a scared expression. He was the scaredest boy I'd ever seen. I walked him back to his house.

Sound of breaking glass!

All Another window!

General murmurs of 'Whose can it be this time?' 'You see anything?' 'No, not mine.' Etc.
Then –

Wendy (*screaming, off stage*) Elvis!

Ruskin Mum! Oh, no! It's our bathroom window! We've only just got it fixed.

Wendy rushes onto street in her (green) dressing gown.

Wendy You see that? Brand new! I can't stand it any more!

Winston rushes out after her.

Winston Calm down.

Wendy Don't tell me to calm down! Oh, Ruskin. What am I going to do?

Suddenly, Ruskin rushes to pub and angrily yells –

Ruskin Stop him! Hear me? Control that son of yours!

Dr Flowers, Mr Lace, Mr Flick, Mrs Walnut, Winston and Wendy, inspired by Ruskin, yell out in a general chorus of –

All Yeah! Ruskin's right. He's turning into trouble. He's ruining this street! He's got to be controlled!

Mr and Mrs Cave appear.
 They are frosty and glaring.

Dr Flowers, Mr Lace, Mr Flick, Mrs Walnut, Winston and Wendy freeze.

Silence.
 Pause.

Then –

Dr Flowers, Mr Lace, Mr Flowers, Mrs Walnut, Winston and Wendy go to their homes.

Ruskin faces Mr and Mrs Cave in silence.
 Slight pause.

Mr Cave You were saying.

Ruskin cannot find his voice.

Mr and Mrs Cave go back into pub.
 Slight pause.

Ruskin . . . I'm a coward.

Corky No.

Ruskin I am! I wanted to be like . . . like Henry V. You know? Give a speech that'll . . . oh, I don't know. Just say what I felt. 'Your son's a bully! And you're bullies too! Mum and Dad don't like going to the pub any more in case you make snide remarks about Dad not having a job. We're all fed up with your, "Ooo, we've just bought

47

a new car!" And, "Ooo, these cigars cost more than
your shoes!" 'Cos bragging about what you've got when
other people ain't got it, that's . . . that's just not
friendly! And it's gotta stop! For the sake of the street!
It's gotta stop!'

Corky claps and cheers.

Corky Bravo, my boy! Bravo!

Ruskin But I didn't say it to them, Corky.

Corky But you *thought* it, my boy. That's the first step.
And one day – who knows? – you might say it, not just
to them, but to the whole world. And when you do . . .
why, I'll be watching you and feeling every bit as proud
as I do now.

Slight pause.

I've got something more to tell you about . . . you know
what.

Ruskin Krindlekrax!

*Ruskin and Corky settle into their armchair-and-cross-
legged-on-floor positions as the scene becomes –*

SCENE TWELVE: CORKY'S LIVING ROOM

Corky is offering Ruskin a plate of biscuits.

Ruskin . . . You've seen it again! When, Corky? Where?

Corky Last night. On the street.

Ruskin But . . . what? How? Was it . . .? I mean, were
you . . .?

Corky Listen! I was in bed. Fast asleep. Suddenly – a jolt
wakes me! As if I'm falling or just tripped up. That ever
happen to you?

Ruskin Yeah, yeah.

Corky My heart's pounding. I lay back and – there! At my window!

Ruskin What?

Corky An eye! A big, red eye. Staring at me. I could see myself reflected in that gigantic eye. Petrified! That's how I looked. Scared to death!

Ruskin Wh . . . what happened?

Corky The creature made a snorting noise and – Wooosh! The eye vanished. Then – clunk!

Ruskin The drain cover!

Corky Exactly, my boy. The creature had gone back down into the sewers. By the time I got to the window . . . Nothing!

Ruskin But . . . how?

Corky What d'you mean?

Ruskin If Krindlekrax is so big –

Corky Huge, my boy! Tyrannosaurus Rex!

Ruskin But the drain cover ain't Tyrannosaurus Rex size.

Corky The cracks in the road, my dear boy! Look round the drain cover. Huge cracks! As Krindlekrax emerges

down the street? Oh, Corky, it might want to eat you!

Corky Goodness, that imagination of yours.

Ruskin But it could be the reason –

Corky Shush, my dear boy. I'm sure we're all perfectly safe. Besides, you and I have every reason to be grateful to Krindlekrax. After all, it was because of Krindlekrax I left the sewers.

Ruskin So?

Corky And had to find another job.

Ruskin School caretaker!

Corky And we became friends.

Ruskin Well, we'd always been friends.

Corky Well, of course. Like everyone on Lizard Street.

Ruskin But when you started working at the school we became –

Corky (*with Ruskin*) Always and for ever friends!

Ruskin (*with Corky*) Always and for ever friends!

   Slight pause.

Corky You know, I used to think children saw me as . . . well, that silly old caretaker. No, no, it's true. They were always very polite, of course. 'Good morning, Corky,' and 'Goodnight, Corky.' But they never really talked to me. And then . . . oh, I remember that day Elvis walked up to me and –

Ruskin Elvis!

Corky But . . . well, he was the first one to talk to me, my boy.

Ruskin You don't have to keep reminding me.

Corky I don't keep –

Ruskin Everything's Elvis! Elvis! Elvis! We might as well name the place Elvis Street. So Elvis spoke to you first. So what? It was me who spoke to you next. And it was me who became your best friend! Don't see Elvis sitting here listening to your boring stories, do you?

Corky Boring?

Ruskin I'm going home! Before you start talking about Elvis again!

Corky Oh, don't go like this. Please. My mum used to say, 'Never go to bed on an argument.'

Ruskin Then you shouldn't've talked about Elvis.

Turns away.

Corky My boy!

Ruskin walks straight into –

SCENE THIRTEEN: RUSKIN'S KITCHEN

Winston is slumped at the table, surrounded by empty cans of lager.
He is wearing an old (and now somewhat frayed) dark green, zookeeper's uniform.
In front of him is a row of toy animals.

Ruskin There is no snake, Dad.

Winston What's this, then?

Picks up a particularly unconvincing toy snake.

A grapefruit?

Ruskin It's a toy, Dad. A toy. You don't work at the zoo any more. You lost your job years ago.

Winston A live mouse. That's what the snake eats. I drop the mouse into the tank and then – oh, I always run, Rusk. Can't watch something like that.

Ruskin Let's get you upstairs, Dad.

Winston Before I hose the elephants? Don't be ridiculous!

Ruskin Dad! Sober up! You. Are. Not. A. Zoo. Keeper.

Winston I'm . . . not?

Ruskin You. Got. Fired.

Winston I . . . I . . . did, didn't I?

Ruskin Yes.

Winston Oh, my beautiful job. The animals . . . oh, how they loved me. Every morning the lions would roar when they saw me. Peacocks would open their feathers.

Ruskin Come on, Dad. Up you –

Winston It's all my fault! You know that, don't you, Rusk? All my fault.

Ruskin If you say so.

Winston I should never have taken that baby crocodile.

Ruskin stares at Winston.

Ruskin The . . . what?

Winston The baby crocodile. I took it, you know.

Ruskin Took it? You mean . . . from the zoo?

Winston I wanted friends, you see.

Ruskin No. I don't . . . see at all, Dad.

Winston Nor do I. Not any more. But it all made a . . . sort of sense at the time. I thought, if I take the baby crocodile, then Mr Cave will like me.

Ruskin Mr Cave! Oh, Dad, what happened?

Winston Oh, it's ancient history now, Ruskin.

Ruskin It's not! At least . . . it might not be. Oh, tell me, Dad. Please. Why would a baby crocodile make Mr Cave like you? Sit down. Come on. Why?

Ruskin helps Winston to sit.
  Slight pause.

Winston He didn't want a baby crocodile. Not at first. The crocodile was my idea. You see, I went into the pub for a drink after work. I was sitting alone as usual. At my little table in the corner.

The light has changed to suggest a pub. A spotlight reveals Mr Cave wiping a glass with a towel. He looks younger, slimmer and – perhaps more alarmingly – has a full head of hair, styled in a quiff.

Mr Cave When was that? The Jurassic period?

Mrs Cave I'll thump you one.

Mr and Mrs Cave canoodle with sickening lovey-doveyness.

Mrs Cave Love you, Hubby.

Mr Cave Love you, Wifey.

Mrs Cave Don't forget the Little One.

Pats belly.

Mr Cave Love you, Little One.

Ruskin That's Elvis in there!

Dr Flowers If you're serious about refurbishment, the sign is the first thing you should attend to. It's an eyesore!

A younger Dr Flowers is now revealed: a head full of hair, ridiculously young.

Mrs Cave What's that?

Mr Cave Eh, Doc?

Dr Flowers Outside. The pub sign. The painting of the Dragon. It's faded so much you can barely see it.

Mr Lace Dr Flowers is right.

Mr Lace is now revealed: like the others, disturbingly younger.

Dr Flowers Thank you, Mr Lace.

Mr Lace That Dragon is where Lizard Street gets its name. A vital piece of our history. It's what attracted you-know-who – to take a break from Stratford-on-Avon and live here for a while.

Mr Cave Who d'ya mean?

Mr Lace You know! The Poet of all Our Hearts. Inventor of the Human. The Magician Of Words.

Mr Cave Oh! You mean Shakesp –

Mr Flick Don't!

A young Mr Flick is now revealed.

Mr Lace Thank you, Mr Flick.

Mr Flick A gin and tonic, if you please. And I agree – the pub sign lets the whole street down. How can I be expected to attract blockbuster film premières if the street looks shoddy?

Mr Cave pours Mr Flick a gin and tonic.

Mrs Cave Shoddy, eh?

Mr Lace A little harsh.

Mr Cave No, no, he's right. A totally new sign! That's what we need! Then after you've had your fancy premières, the audiences will come here and –

Mrs Cave Guzzle a fortune!

Mr Cave I'll paint it right away.

Mr Flick You?

Mr Cave Why not?

Mr Flick Except a magnolia wall.

Mr Lace Exactly.

Mr Cave Well . . . I can copy things. Drew a greyhound at school. My mate had one. Teacher said it was very realistic.

Mrs Cave In case you hadn't noticed, hubby o' mine, mates with dragons are a little thinner on the ground.

Mr Cave What ya getting at?

Mr Flick You can't copy one.

Mr Lace Why don't you find something that has a *resemblance* to a Dragon?

Mr Cave Like what?

Slight pause.

Winston . . . A crocodile?

Everyone looks at Winston.
Slight pause.

Mr Cave Well, yeah. A crocodile. But I told you before, Winston, I ain't paying good money to visit that zoo of yours. I see enough strange animals in here every night – Ha! Ha! Ha!

No one else laughs.
Slight pause.

So . . . what ya gonna do, Winston? Drag a twenty-foot crocodile home for me?

Everyone laughs.

Winston No. But I can carry a baby one.

Everyone stops laughing.

Mr Cave Go on.

Winston We've got a baby crocodile. Bright green and the size of a shoe. I could easily sneak it out.

56

Slowly, led by Mr Cave, the others cluster round Winston.

Winston It's brilliant to look at! Red eyes!

Mr Cave Big tail?

Winston Yeah, yeah.

Mrs Cave Sharp claws?

Winston Like razors.

Dr Flowers An ideal dragon substitute, I'd say.

Mr Flick They used to use reptiles as dinosaurs in old films, you know.

Winston You can have it for a whole night.

Mrs Cave Oh . . . Hubby! Do you think you could do it?

Mr Cave Do anything, me! Anyone doubt it? Eh?

Mr Lace It'll be a masterpiece, I'm sure.

Mr Flick A classic.

Mrs Cave It better be.

Mr Cave Let me get you a drink, Winston.

Winston Oh, Ruskin . . . I was so happy that night.

Mr Cave, Mrs Cave, Mr Lace, Dr Flowers and

Lights come up on an illuminated glass reptile tank with baby crocodile inside.

Winston There it is.

Warily, attempts to grab the crocodile.
The crocodile snaps its jaws.
Winston jumps back.

Winston tries again.
Again the crocodile snaps.

Ruskin is watching carefully and –

Ruskin Now, Dad!

Winston grabs crocodile.
He puts it into small canvas bag.

Ruskin (*with Winston*) Yesss!!

Winston (*with Ruskin*) Yesss!!

Glass tank dims.
Spotlight on Mr Cave.

Mr Cave A crocodile! What a mate you are!

Winston I need it back by morning.

Mr Cave Yeah, yeah.

Winston I'll be here at six-thirty . . . Okay? You listening?

Mr Cave walks away, looking in bag.

Winston You hear me? Hello? Hello?

Ruskin Did Mr Cave paint it?

Winston Oh, yes. The sign you see on the pub now is – oh, that's the very crocodile. But that night . . . oh, it all went wrong! Horribly, horribly wrong.

Ruskin How, Dad? How?

Winston A siren woke me up.

Ruskin A siren?

Winston Ambulance. And then –

Mrs Cave (*screaming, off*) Ahhhhhhh!

Ruskin Mrs Cave!

Winston She's having the baby.

Ruskin Elvis!

Winston The ambulance has come for her! But . . . my crocodile. My crocodile!

Mr Cave is now revealed, agitated.

Mr Cave I'm having a baby! Having a baby!

Winston Where is it?

Mr Cave Don't you know where babies come from?

Winston My crocodile!

Mr Cave Your what?

Winston Crocodile! Crocodile! Croco –

Mr Cave Oh, yeah! That! I did the painting. Thanks. Now I've got to get going! My head's spinning! I'm having a baby. Having a –

Winston But where is it?

her dressing gown.

Winston Mr Gave he cave you – Mr Gave he cave –

Mrs Walnut What? What? Calm down.

Winston Mr Cave gave you – gave you to look after –

Mrs Walnut Something in a bag! Yes. He put it on the table. Here it is . . .

   Picks up empty bag.

Oh!

Winston It's gone!

Mrs Walnut Must've fallen out.

Winston Crawled out!

Mrs Walnut *Crawled?* What . . . what on earth was it?

Winston The street door's open! It could've gone anywhere! Anywhere!

   Mrs Walnut fades into darkness.

Winston All night long I searched. Behind every dustbin. Under every car. Nothing! The baby crocodile was nowhere to be seen. I searched until the sun was coming up and I heard –

   Spotlight on Mr Cave.

Mr Cave I HAVE A SON!

   Lights cigar.

Ruskin Elvis is born!

   Others are revealed, cheering, etc.

   Mr Cave passes cigars around.

Winston My job is lost. Everything is lost.

   Cheering from crowd fades away.
   Pause.

Ruskin The sewers!

Winston What?

Ruskin That's where it went, Dad. The crocodile. And it – oh, it grew and grew into . . . No! Mustn't tell, Dad. Sorry. Promised.

Winston What are you going on about, Rusk?

Ruskin Corky! Got to tell Corky. Not now. Too late. He'll be asleep. And the argument. Oh, no! The argument. My fault. Oh, Corky, sorry.

Winston is gazing at Ruskin, bewildered.

Winston . . . Time for bed, I think.

Gets to his feet, stumbles.

Ruskin rushes to help him.

Ruskin Careful, Dad.

Winston You're a good son, Rusk. You know that? The bestest son in the whole world.

They make their way upstairs.
Slowly, lights fade to darkness.
Darkness for a while.
Then –

window box. Then he notices Corky –

Dr Flowers Corky!

Rushes over and feels Corky's pulse, etc.
    Slight pause.

Mr Lace comes out of his house.
    He takes a deep breath of fresh air.
    Then notices Dr Flowers with Corky –

Mr Lace Corky!

Rushes over to Corky and Dr Flowers.
    Dr Flowers shakes his head.
    Mr Lace lets out a gasp.
    Slight pause.

Mr Flick comes out of cinema.
    He admires the front of his establishment.
    Then notices Dr Flowers and Mr Lace with Corky –

Mr Flick Corky!

Rushes to Corky.
    Dr Flowers and Mr Lace shake their heads.
    Mr Flick lets out a gasp.
    Slight pause.

Mrs Walnut comes out of grocer's.
    She starts to prepare for opening.
    Then notices Dr Flowers, Mr Lace and Mr Flick
with Corky –

Mrs Walnut Corky!

Rushes over.
    Dr Flowers, Mr Lace and Mr Flick shake their
heads.
    Mrs Walnut lets out a gasp.
    Slight pause.

Mr Cave and Mrs Cave come out of the pub.
    They start to put up more posters for Elvis.
    Then notice the others with Corky –

Mr Cave (*with Mrs Cave*) Corky!

Mrs Cave (*with Mr Cave*) Corky!

Mr and Mrs Cave rush over to Corky.
The others shake their heads.
Mr and Mrs Cave gasp.
Slight pause.

Wendy comes out of her house.
She goes to put toast down the drain.
Then notices the crowd and –

Wendy Corky!

Rushes over.

The others shake their heads.
Wendy cries out as –

Ruskin leaves house, carrying satchel.

Ruskin Morning, everyone . . .

The others try to shield Corky from him.

Ruskin Wh . . . what's going on? What . . .? Mum?

Wendy Oh, Ruskin . . .

Ruskin Corky! Corky!

Rushes over.

Stares at Corky.

Slight pause.

Dr Flowers A heart attack, by the looks of it.

Mr Flick Must've happened just as he left the house.

Mr Lace Goodnight, sweet Corky, and flights of angels sing thee to thy rest.

Ruskin is now kneeling by the body and, very softly –

Ruskin Corky . . .?

Gently touches Corky.

Wake up, Corky. It's me.

Winston comes out of house, hangover-groggy.

Wendy Winston . . .

Winston approaches crowd.

Mrs Walnut There's nothing you can do, Ruskin.

Ruskin Corky. I've got things to tell you.

Winston Come on, son.

Ruskin But Dad . . . Corky doesn't know the rest of the story. Corky! Corky!

Ruskin is hysterical now.

Others try to hold him.

Ruskin Corky! I've got to talk to him. Let me go!

Struggles free.

Wendy Oh, Ruskin. Please. Don't.

Elvis and Sparkey now appear.
They watch from a distance in silence.

Ruskin He wouldn't leave me. He wouldn't . . . wouldn't want to. I know he wouldn't.

Winston It's not my fault.

Mr Cave It's no one's fault.

Ruskin It is! Don't you see that? It's *all* your fault! Krindlekrax got him!

Mr Lace He's gone hysterical now.

Ruskin I'm not! Krindlekrax got him. And Krindlekrax is all your faults! It's *your* fault –

Points at Dr Flowers.

– because you said the pub needed a new sign. And it's *your* fault –

Points at Mr Flick.

– because you agreed. And it's *your* fault –

Points at Mr Cave.

– because you said you'd paint it! And it's *your* fault –

Points at Mr Lace.

– because you said paint something that looks like a dragon. And it's *your* fault –

Points at Winston.

– because you stole a baby crocodile! And it's *your* fault –

the drain. That's what it probably feeds on. The whole

street is to blame! And I'll never forgive you! Never!
I HATE YOU, LIZARD STREET! I HATE YOU!
I HATE YOU!

> *Ruskin is backing away from them.*
> *Now he climbs into bed and the scene becomes –*

SCENE FIFTEEN: RUSKIN'S BEDROOM

Ruskin is in bed.
  He is drained with grief.
  He is holding Corky's walking stick and helmet.
A medal is also on the bed.

*On the bedside cabinet are an undrunk cup of tea and
uneaten plate of toast.*

Pause.

Wendy enters, clutching plate of toast and cup of tea.

Wendy Ruskin?

Ruskin . . . Mmmm?

Wendy I've bought you some toast and – oh, look!

> *Indicates bedside cabinet.*

You haven't touched what I left this afternoon. You've
got to eat.

Ruskin Why?

> *Wendy puts toast and tea on cabinet, then sits on edge
> of mattress.*

Wendy You can't carry on like this.

Ruskin Why?

Wendy Well . . . Corky wouldn't want it.

66

Ruskin Why?

Wendy Because he loved you.

Slight pause.

Everything dies, Rusk.

Ruskin Why?

Wendy It's . . . nature.

Ruskin Well, nature's not . . . natural!

Slight pause.

Wendy We thought you might like this.

Hands Ruskin golden medal.

Ruskin What is it?

Wendy Corky's medal.

Ruskin What did he get it for?

Wendy I don't know. No one does. Whenever it was
mentioned Corky always said, 'Oh, I did nothing really.
Nothing at all.' You know how modest he was. He never
told anyone.

Ruskin He would've told me. Oh, no one misses him
like I do.

Wendy You're wrong.

Ruskin A star? You?

Wendy I wasn't always what I am now, Rusk. Once . . . once I was a pretty young woman. A pretty young woman with dreams. Who sang in a pub.

Ruskin A pub?

Wendy Yes. Mr Cave's pub. Although it wasn't Mr Cave's pub then. It belonged to Mrs Cave. She was the landlord's daughter. It was she who hired me. Oh, it was such a happy time. When I close my eyes I can still . . . The spotlight! My beautiful green dress! The sequins! The cheers! Applause! Yes, Corky! You're right! I can be a star!

Ruskin So . . . what happened?

Wendy Oh, it . . . it don't matter now.

Ruskin It does!

Slight pause.

Mum! Tell me! Look – I'll eat my toast!

Starts eating toast.

Wendy . . . Mr Cave asked me to marry him.

Ruskin Mr Cave! You!

Nearly chokes.

Wendy He was my Number One Fan. Every Saturday night – there he'd be. Front row. With his best mate. Winston.

Ruskin Dad! Mr Cave! You never told me . . . *no one* ever told me this.

Wendy What's the point? What's done is done. And I've said too much now . . .

Ruskin No! Mum! Please!

Slight pause.

68

Wendy I said 'yes' to Mr Cave. He was over the moon. *I* was over the moon. And then Winston – your dad – your *future* dad – he said he was up for promotion at work.

Ruskin At the zoo?

Wendy He'd be Chief Zoo Keeper at . . . Zoo Hollywood.

Ruskin Hollywood! Oh, Mum!

Wendy He asked me to marry him too. And I thought, if I do . . . I could go to Hollywood.

Ruskin Get a singing job!

Wendy Get an agent!

Ruskin Make a film!

Wendy A hit film!

Ruskin Be a star!

Wendy So what should I do? Tell me, Rusk. Marry Mr Cave or your dad?

Ruskin Dad.

Wendy One year later – five days before your dad's promotion was due to happen – he got fired. Why? No one ever found out. At least, I didn't. Mr Cave married Mrs Cave. And me? I was stuck here in Number One

Ruskin and Wendy embrace.

Slight pause.

Now, finish your toast.

Ruskin Yes, Mum.

Wendy Kiss me goodnight.

Ruskin It's not bedtime yet.

Wendy I'm having an early night.

Ruskin Don't you feel well?

Wendy No, no, I'm fine. It's just that . . . well, I haven't been sleeping very well these last few nights.

Ruskin Thinking about Corky?

Wendy And worrying about you. Though why that should give me nightmares about a giant crocodile I've no idea.

Ruskin Giant crocodile!

Wendy It's just a silly nightmare, Rusk.

Ruskin Tell me about it, Mum. Then I'll finish my toast.

Wendy Well . . . A big, red eye! That's what I saw. A big, red eye, staring at me through the bedroom window. I was so scared I couldn't move. Then . . . the eye goes away. I see a glimpse of green skin. Sharp teeth. Swish of tail. Then I scream and – awake! In bed. Staring at the window. Just like in the dream. Oh, it all feels so . . . so . . . real. Not a dream at all. Even when I'm awake I can smell the creature.

Ruskin What does it smell like?

Wendy Like . . . like your dad's smelly socks.

Kisses Ruskin.

Goodnight, love.

Ruskin What –? Oh, yeah. 'Night, Mum.

Wendy leaves.

Ruskin Krindlekrax! . . . You hear that, fellow thespians? Krindlekrax is staring at Mum. Just like it stared at . . . oh! Perhaps Krindlekrax is after Mum! Perhaps the whole street! Dr Flowers! Mr Lace! Mr Flick! Mrs Walnut! Mr and Mrs Cave! Elvis! Sparkey! Everyone. Oh, someone's got to stop Krindlekrax before it's too late! Someone's got to go down to the sewers and say, 'I'm not afraid of you!'

Puts Corky's helmet on.

Me! It's . . . it's got to be me! No one else knows. It was our secret. Me and Corky. I'm the only one who can do it.

Picks up Corky's walking stick.

I've got to save Lizard Street. Got to be a hero. Like Corky was.

Pins Corky's medal on.

Tonight! When the street sleeps . . .

Lighting turns from sunset to moonlight and the scene becomes –

SCENE SIXTEEN: LIZARD STREET

oh, Corky, I wish you was with me . . . wish anyone was with me . . .

Turns helmet light on.

I can do this! I'm a hero! Krindlekrax! You don't scare me!

Starts to climb down drain.

I'm coming to get you, Krindlekrax. Ruskin Splinter's gonna tame you once and for all! Hear me, Krindlekrax? Hear me?

As Ruskin disappears down drain –

Blackout and –

Krindlekrax (*over speakers, deafeningly loud*)
RAAAAAAAHHHHHHH!!!!!

Act Two

SCENE SEVENTEEN: THE SEWER

Green, rippling light.
  The sound of dripping and trickling.
  Every drip and trickle is vast and echoing.
  The rest . . . darkness, silence.

Ruskin appears, his torchlight cutting through the gloom.
  He is clutching the walking stick like a sword.
  Any confidence he once exuded has all but disappeared now.

Ruskin (*calling*) K–K–Krindlekrax!

  Slight pause.

K–K–Krindlekrax!

  Pause

K–Krin . . . Oh, Corky! I never imaged the sewers would be so –

  Rats scamper by.

Ahhh! Oh, Corky! Everything's just much . . . more!

transformed yourself in every part you played. Sometimes

I didn't even recognise you. Brave soldiers, brave kings, brave knights. They were all you. Yet you were just a grey-haired old wimp – Sorry, sorry. But you know what I mean. And that's exactly what I've got to do. Transform myself into . . . something brave.

More rats scamper by.

Ahhh! Oh, how can I start acting like a hero? What're your thespian tips? The walk! That's right! You once said building a character starts with how they walk . . . Mmmm, let's see . . . Hal Oaktree has strong legs . . . Mmm . . . Bulky muscles in calves and thighs so – big strides! Yes! Chest out! Bit of a swagger. I'm confident. No one will get in my way.

Starts practising walk.

Dr Flowers I'm not convinced.

Dr Flowers is now revealed. He is dressed in his daytime clothes, perfectly relaxed and – in this setting – perfectly incongruous.

Ruskin Dr Flowers! How . . . how did you get down here?

Dr Flowers Remember what Corky said? About the smell getting in his head?

Ruskin You mean . . . you're a hallucination! Wow!

Dr Flowers Doesn't stop me having an opinion, Ruskin. And your hero act . . . Well, can I be a plain-speaking hallucination?

Ruskin Go ahead.

Dr Flowers It makes the sewer smell like a rose garden.

Slight pause.

Oh, Ruskin. I'm sorry. But you've got to realise that . . . well, just because we might *want* to be something, doesn't means we're going to *be* it. Take me for instance. Do you think I wanted to be a family doctor?

Ruskin Didn't you?

Dr Flowers Certainly not. When I was your age, I wanted to be a botanical explorer. Travelling the world in search of exotic plants. The *Victoria regina*, for instance. Know what that is? Oh, what a plant! A giant water lily from the Amazon. Its white and pink leaves are the size of a mattress and strong enough to support a child. Oh, how I would've loved to have discovered such a wonder.

Ruskin So . . . why didn't you?

Dr Flowers My dad. He was the doctor on Lizard Street when I was a child. Everyone loved Dad. 'We're safe in Doctor Flowers' hands,' they'd say. And then . . . well, Dad got sick. I started to help out in the surgery. Little jobs at first. Taking temperatures. Counting tablets. Measuring medication. Next thing I knew, Dad was dead, the surgery was mine and . . . goodbye, *Victoria regina*, hello, Lizard Street for the rest of my life.

Ruskin Don't you like Lizard Street?

Dr Flowers 'Course I do. It's home, Ruskin. All my friends are here. Although down here is a bit . . . well, spooky, don't you think?

and follow me home.

Walks away.

Ruskin goes to follow, then hesitates.

Dr Flowers Come on. You know you want to.

Ruskin No. I won't. Go away! Leave me alone!

Dr Flowers fades into darkness.

Ruskin I can be a hero! I can! Corky told me!

Looks at photo.

First – the walk! Then . . . what? The voice! Yes! A hero
should have a commanding one . . . 'Hello, I am hero
Ruskin Splinter and I –'

Mr Lace Don't call us, we'll call you.

*Mr Lace is revealed. He is dressed in his daytime
clothes, perfectly relaxed and – in the circumstances –
perfectly incongruous.*

Ruskin Mr Lace!

Mr Lace How'd I get here? Anyone?

Ruskin's hand shoots up.

Ruskin Hallucination caused by smelly-sock stink, sir.

Mr Lace Correct. And can hallucinations have opinions?

Ruskin's hand shoots up.

Ruskin They can, sir.

Mr Lace Correct!

Ruskin Have you got an opinion, sir?

Mr Lace I have.

Ruskin Is it about my acting?

Mr Lace It is.

Ruskin Can I hear it, please?

Mr Lace Ruskin, your acting is so bad it makes me lose the will to live.

Ruskin What you trying to say, Mr Lace?

Mr Lace Oh, don't torture yourself, Ruskin. All the world might well be a stage but . . . well, some of us are destined to merely sweep it.

Ruskin And you think . . . I'm a sweeper?

Mr Lace Somewhere there's a broom with your name on it.

Slight pause.

Oh, Ruskin, I'm sorry. I know what it's like to want something. Want it with all your heart, yet have it remain just beyond your reach. I remember the day my mum took me to the theatre for the first time. I was eight years old. I didn't want to go. Oh, the foolishness of youth. But Mum – that determined Titania – she tempted me with promises of a taxi ride and a big bar of chocolate. So I went. Sat in my seat in the auditorium. Not very comfortable. I moaned. And then – oh, the lights dimmed. Curtains parted. And there! On the stage! Magical moonlight! A forest! Fairies! A changeling child! . . . What was the play? Anyone?

Ruskin *A Midsummer Night's Dream*, sir.

children. I am their guru! They worship me! Worship!

Ruskin But . . . they don't.

Mr Lace . . . No. Theatres laughed at my concept of an Irish dancing *Othello*. I never got the chance to put any of my ideas into practice. I have achieved . . . naught.

Ruskin Not true. You're a fantastic teacher.

Mr Lace It was only going to be a part-time job, you know. Two days a week while I pursued my real passion. But when my Amish *Coriolanus* came to nothing . . . well, two days became three. Then four. Then . . . I am Mr Lace, teacher at Lizard Street School. And you are not my audience, you are my pupil.

Ruskin Your best!

Mr Lace In some subjects.

Ruskin Drama! English! I always get A-minus in those.

Mr Lace But you get A-plus in one subject.

Ruskin What?

Mr Lace Wimp!

   Slight pause.

Oh, Ruskin, Ruskin, stop all this foolishness. You're not meant to be down here. You should be tucked up in bed . . . Come on. Follow me home. You know you want to . . . Follow me . . . Follow me . . .

   Ruskin starts to follow.
    Then –

Ruskin No! Won't!

Mr Lace But Ruskin –

Ruskin Go away! Go away!

   Mr Lace fades into darkness.

Ruskin I can be a hero! I'm *sure* of it!

Looks at photo.

Sir Alec! You've got to give me more hints. How can I do it? Eh? If I can't . . . well, if I can't actually feel like a hero, then can you teach me how to . . . fake it?

Mr Flick Mr Hitchcock!

Mr Flick is revealed, clutching his torch. He is dressed in his daytime clothes, perfectly relaxed and – in these circumstances – perfectly incongruous.

Ruskin Mr Flick!

Mr Flick 'Fake it!' That's what Mr Hitchcock said – the film director. You know?

Ruskin Of course.

Mr Flick He was directing an actress – oh, what was her name?

Ruskin Ingrid Bergman.

Mr Flick Miss Bergman! Of course. And Mr Hitchcock was trying to direct her and Miss Bergman said, 'Oh, really, Hitch. I can't do that. I don't feel it.' And Mr Hitchcock said –

Ruskin 'My dear Ingrid, just fake it.'

Ruskin Spit it out!

Mr Flick You're pants!

Slight pause.

Oh, Ruskin. I'm sorry. But if you can't convince me – and, as you know, I'm one of your biggest fans – then . . . well, you're never going to be able to convince –

Ruskin Alright, alright.

Mr Flick We can't always achieve our dreams, you know. I used to dream of owning a huge cinema complex. Twenty screens. Ear-blasting sound.

Ruskin Don't tell me! You applied for jobs. They turned you down. You gave up trying. Settled for . . . Flick's Ritz. Motto of the story being?

Mr Flick Go back to bed, Ruskin.

Ruskin Knew it.

Mr Flick Follow me.

Ruskin No. I won't, Mr Flick. You hear? I'm . . . I'm still sure I can be a hero.

Mr Flick Just imagine your nice, soft mattress, all safe and –

Ruskin Not listening.

Mr Flick Oh, Ruskin, the blankets tucked around you –

Ruskin La-de-la-di-dah –

Mrs Walnut Chocky-bicky?

Mrs Walnut is revealed, clutching packet of chocolate biscuits. She is dressed in her daytime clothes, perfectly relaxed and – in these circumstances – perfectly incongruous.

Ruskin Oh, not another one!

Mrs Walnut You ain't had one yet!

Ruskin Hallucination, I mean.

Mrs Walnut They're digestives.

Ruskin Oh, very funny. Listen, they're not real. Just like you.

Mrs Walnut Me! Are you telling me that I'm no more real than this digestive? Well, I've had a lot of insults thrown at me in my time, but that takes the biscuit. Ha!

Mr Flick Ha!

Mrs Walnut That was a joke, Ruskin.

Mr Flick He's in a terrible mood.

Mrs Walnut Why's that?

Ruskin Because I know what you're going to say.

Mrs Walnut Oh, mind-reader now, are we?

Ruskin 'You're not a hero, Ruskin. You're a wimp. Your acting's pants. Forget the whole thing. Follow me home.' Right?

Mrs Walnut I would never say something so hurtful.

Ruskin You will.

Mrs Walnut Won't.

Ruskin Will.

wanted to . . . what? Own a chain of supermarkets or

something? Travel from store to store in a big Rolls-Royce?

Mrs Walnut What a ridiculous idea. I'm perfectly happy with my little grocery shop.

Ruskin You . . . are?

Mr Flick Don't say it like that! Mrs Walnut's shop is perfectly charming.

Mrs Walnut Thank you, Mr Flick. I had my first kiss in that shop – Oh, do you mind de-hallucinating Mr Flick for this, Ruskin?

Mr Flick No, no, I want to hear –

Fades into darkness.

Mrs Walnut His name was Alf. Oh . . . Alf! The shop belonged to his dad. I used to help out on Saturday mornings. Only did it because of Alf, of course. Love at first sight it was. For me, at least. The way the potato dust stuck on his hairy arms. Like pollen. And I was the bee that came along and . . . buzz-buzz. Oh, we made such honey!

Ruskin So . . . where is this Alf now?

Mrs Walnut He left me. Two days after Sparkey was born. Took one look at the baby and –

Ruskin Buzzed off!

Mrs Walnut It's not funny, Ruskin.

Ruskin . . . Sorry.

Mrs Walnut He sent me a postcard. From some island miles away. Said he couldn't bear being trapped by life on Lizard Street any more. Me! A trap? His own son! A trap? I couldn't believe it! Every day I read it . . . and it still makes no sense. Oh . . . how I miss the potato pollen on his arms . . . I miss . . . I miss . . .

Stifles a tear.

Ruskin Don't talk about it if it upsets you.

Mrs Walnut No. It helps to talk. But . . . oh, not here, Ruskin. The smell is quite revolting. Let's go back home. There's so much more I want to tell you. Come on. Chocky-bickies and a cup of tea, eh? Wouldn't you like that?

Ruskin I . . . would, yeah.

Mrs Walnut Come on, then.

Ruskin starts to follow.
Then –

Ruskin Hang on! You're just trying to get me out of the sewer like everyone else. Well . . . clear off! You can't fool me! *I'm* staying! *You* disappear!

Mrs Walnut Not yet, Ruskin. Please!

Ruskin Yes!

Mrs Walnut begins to fade into darkness . . .

Mrs Walnut No, Ruskin. Don't. I've got to convince you . . . oh, help! Help!

Mr Cave (*with Mrs Cave*) Bring her back!

Mrs Cave (*with Mr Cave*) Bring her back!

Mr Cave You heard, Ruskin.

Mrs Cave (*with Mr Cave*) Now!

Mr Cave (*with Mrs Cave*) Now!

  Mrs Walnut is, once again, fully illuminated.

Mrs Walnut Chocky-bicky? Chocky-bicky?

Mrs Cave What are you playing at, you silly woman?

Mrs Walnut Tempting him home.

Mr Cave He needs more than chocky-bickies for that.

Mrs Cave He needs plain talking.

Mr Cave Ruskin! You're a wimp!

Mrs Cave A weed!

Mr Cave A mouse!

Mrs Walnut A worm!

Mr Cave This is no place for you.

Mrs Cave Go home!

Mr Cave Now!

Ruskin But . . . but . . .

Mr Cave Just look at ya! Trembling with fear!

Mrs Cave More nervous than a chihuahua in a cement-mixer.

Mr Cave A chihuahua's got more bottle.

Mrs Walnut A carton of milk's got more bottle.

Mrs Cave I've got pimples with more courage.

Mr Cave My dandruff's got more muscles.

Mrs Cave Face it, Ruskin!

Mr Cave Face it, Ruskin!

Mrs Walnut Face it, Ruskin!

All (*except Ruskin*) YOU ARE NOT A HERO!

Ruskin I . . . am. I . . . I . . . I'm br-brave and –

Elvis BOO!

> *Elvis is abruptly revealed, clutching ball. He is dressed in his daytime clothes, perfectly relaxed and – in these circumstances – perfectly incongruous.*
>
> *Ruskin jumps and cries out at Elvis's 'BOO!'*

Mr Cave Ha!

Mrs Cave Ha!

Mrs Walnut Nice one, Elvis.

Ruskin Nice one? You said you'd give Sparkey anti-Elvis tablets.

Mrs Walnut I did not.

Ruskin You did!

Elvis Wanna be friends again, Rusk?

Ruskin Wh . . . what?

Elvis You and me. Mates. Like before.

Ruskin No . . . head-scratching?

Mrs Cave What you waiting for?

Mr Cave You want to be friends with Elvis again, don't you?

Elvis We can play games together. Watch telly. Muck about. Oh, come on, Rusk. Don't you miss all that?

Ruskin 'Course I do.

Elvis So . . . you wanna be friends again? Yeah or nah?

Ruskin . . . Yeah!

Elvis Then all you have to do is say, 'I am not a hero and I wanna go home.'

Ruskin But I . . . I am a –

Elvis Nah. You ain't.

Ruskin Could be.

Sparkey BOO!

Sparkey is abruptly revealed. He is dressed in daytime clothes, perfectly relaxed and – in these circumstances – perfectly incongruous.

Ruskin jumps and cries out at Sparkey's 'BOO!'

Mrs Walnut That's my boy!

Ruskin Stop it! Please! All of you!

Mrs Cave Place getting to you, eh, Ruskin?

Dr Flowers The dark?

Mr Lace The smell?

Mr Flick The rats?

Dr Flowers, Mr Lace and Mr Flick are revealed once more.

Mr Cave And worse.

Mrs Cave Much worse.

Elvis The worst. Right, Sparkey?

Sparkey Right.

Ruskin Wh . . . what d'you mean?

All (*except Ruskin*) Krindlekrax.

Dr Flowers With claws!

Mr Lace Sharp teeth!

Mrs Walnut Red eyes!

Mr Cave Oh, Ruskin. Stop struggling to be something you ain't.

Mrs Cave Tell him, Wendy.

Mr Cave Tell him, Winston.

Wendy and Winston are now revealed. They are dressed in their daytime clothes, perfectly relaxed and – in these circumstances – perfectly incongruous.

Wendy (*with Winston*) Be like us.

Winston (*with Wendy*) Be like us.

Wendy Forget dreams.

Mr Cave Say it, Ruskin.

They all start closing in on Ruskin.

Mrs Cave Say it.

Dr Flowers Say it.

Mr Lace Say it.

Mr Flick Say it

Mrs Walnut Say it.

Elvis Say it.

Sparkey Say it.

Wendy Say it.

Winston Say it.

Ruskin I . . . I'm . . . not a hero . . .

All (*except Ruskin*) Mmmm?

Ruskin And . . . I wanna go home.

They all applaud Ruskin, cheer, slap his back, etc.

Mr Cave I'm proud of you.

Mrs Cave Me too.

Mr Lace We all are.

Elvis Mates again?

Ruskin . . . Yeah.

Sparkey I'm so happy.

Ruskin Me too.

Elvis Me too.

Mr Cave We're all happy!

Mr Lace Euphoric!

Wendy You see, Ruskin? How easy it is to make everyone happy? Now, come on. Let's go home. You a hero? Ha!

All (*except Ruskin*) Ha!

Winston Come on, Rusk. Follow us.

All (*except Ruskin, gently, haunting*) Follow us . . . follow us . . . follow us . . .

Ruskin (*overlapping*) Yeah . . . What was I thinking of? . . . Could do with a cup of cocoa . . .

Corky STOP!!!

> *Corky is now in spotlight. He is dressed in his daytime clothes, perfectly relaxed and – in these circumstances – perfectly incongruous.*

All (*except Corky*) Corky!

Corky Come here, my boy.

All (*except Ruskin and Corky*) Stay here, Rusk. Stay with us. Don't listen. (*etc.*)

> *Ruskin hesitates.*

Corky Come here . . . my hero!

> *Ruskin rushes to Corky.*

All (*gasping, except for Ruskin and Corky*) No!

be in bed. Come home . . . come home . . .

Ruskin (*overlapping whispering*) I didn't mean it, Corky. They're not boring. Oh, I'm sorry I said that. It's been doing my head in. I'm sorry, I'm sorry.

Corky (*overlapping whispering*) You lost your temper, my boy. That's all. Don't worry about it. I'd forgotten it by the time you closed the front door. All is forgiven. Hear me? When people love each other . . . all is always forgiven.

Others are fading into darkness.

Ruskin Corky! My dad! He stole the baby crocodile and –

Corky I know, I know. Voices from above filter down here to the sewers. I've heard every single thing that's been happening. And I'm here to tell you: You made the right decision, my boy. You are absolutely right to face . . . whatever lies ahead.

Ruskin But that lot kept telling me –

Looks behind.

They're . . . they're gone.

Corky Should hope so too. I'm surprised at you, my dear boy. Cluttering up my sewers with hallucinations like that.

Ruskin I didn't want them here.

Corky Didn't you?

Ruskin No! But . . . I'm glad I'm hallucinating you.

Corky Oh, that's what you're doing, is it?

Ruskin Well . . . yes. How else could you be here? You . . . you died.

Corky gives Ruskin a knowing look.

Ruskin . . . No?

Corky continues to stare.

Ruskin A . . . ghost!

Corky At your service, dear boy.

Ruskin Wow!

Corky Glad you're pleased.

Ruskin Pleased! I'm . . . oh, words can't describe. The others – they were just . . .

Corky Figments of you imagination.

Ruskin Exactly. They told me things . . . well, things I knew but buried in my mind. You know?

Corky Your subconscious.

Ruskin That's it! But you . . . oh, Corky! You're real. In an unreal sort of way. And . . . oh, I'm talking to you again. That's just what I wanted and – Hang on!

Corky What?

Ruskin If . . . if I did hallucinate you then I'd want that hallucination to convince me it wasn't an hallucination because I wouldn't want it to be a hallucination I'd want it to be exactly what you say you are so my subconscious could still be doing it all and giving me a hallucination

Corky Let me tell you something you don't know.

Slight pause.

Ruskin The medal! How'd you get the medal?

Slight pause.

Corky The medal! Very good! Listen . . . When I was a child – about your age – there was a great battle.

Ruskin The Second World War.

Corky Correct, my dear boy. I remember the sound of aircraft approaching. Rushing to the shelters. Then – booom! Oh, the ground shook. And, later, things burning . . . houses turned to rubble . . . So sad, so sad.

Slight pause.

Ruskin Go on, Corky. Please.

Corky What celebration! When the war ended. Oh, what a party we had. Lizard Street was full of flags and music. A big table went down the whole street. We had jelly and ice cream and a bar of chocolate each.

Ruskin That was luxury in those days, wasn't it?

Corky A feast! Oh, we children were so happy. We went to play on the dump at the end of the street.

Ruskin The dump?

Corky A bombsite, my boy. Just bricks and broken wood. But for us children . . . oh, it could be anything. A castle. A jungle. I jumped from broken wall to old armchair to burnt staircase to –

Gasps.

Ruskin What?

Corky I've landed on something and . . . oh, I've never seen anything like it before. It's pointed and . . . silver. Like a metal fish head and . . . it's ticking!

Ruskin A bomb!

Corky Afraid so.

Ruskin Don't move!

Corky I won't. If I move . . . it . . . might . . .

Ruskin Boom.

Corky No more Lizard Street. I yell to the other children, 'Run! I'll stay perfectly still. Just . . . oh, get help! Get help!'

Keeps very still.

Ruskin You . . . you couldn't move a muscle, could you?

Corky Not one.

Slight pause.

Ooo, look at that.

Ruskin What?

Corky On my head. A sparrow. And another. And on my hand. You see?

Ruskin Yeah. And you stayed like this until the bomb was defused?

Corky . . . I did.

Ruskin And Lizard Street was saved.

know yourself to be. Remember the sun and moon. What mustn't they do?

Ruskin Doubt.

Corky Exactly. And in your heart – no matter what the rest of the street might say – you mustn't doubt either. You hear me? You must never doubt what you know you really are.

Ruskin I . . . I won't, Corky.

Corky And what are you?

Ruskin A hero.

Corky My boy, it's time to face Krindlekrax.

A subterranean, deep roar begins to fill the auditorium.

Krindlekrax Raaaaahhhhh!

Ruskin spins round in surprise.
  Corky fades into darkness.

Ruskin Corky! Corky!

Krindlekrax (*getting louder, off*) Raaaaaaahhhhh!

Ruskin A hero! I am! Corky said! . . . Come on, Krindlekrax.

Krindlekrax (*offstage*) Raaaaaaahhhhhhh!!

Ruskin Come on! . . . Come up to the street and fight like a real dragon! Come on! I dare you! Come on! I am not afraid!

Krindlekrax (*offstage*) RAAAAAAAHHHHH!!!

Ruskin begins to run into . . .

SCENE EIGHTEEN: LIZARD STREET

Ruskin climbs up from the sewers into the moonlit street.

Krindlekrax (*from below*) RAAAHHHHH!

Ruskin It's getting close . . . I can smell it . . .

Krindlekrax (*from below*) RAAAHHHHH!

Ruskin Its hot breath . . . Like opening an oven . . . I'm not scared! I am a hero!

Krindlekrax (*from below*) RAAAAAHHHH!!

Ruskin 'I am brave . . . and wise and . . .'

> *A roll of thunder.*
> *Flash of lightning.*

Ruskin Oh, no! That's all I need! A storm!

Krindlekrax (*from below, much closer*) RAAAAAAAHHHHHHH!!!

Ruskin Come on! I'm ready! Show yourself, Krindlekrax!

> *A* claw *emerges from the drain.*

> *Ruskin freezes.*
> *Slight pause.*

Flick, Mrs Walnut, Mr Cave, Mrs Cave, Wendy,

Winston, Elvis and Sparkey. They are all within
a structure (complete with sharp teeth, red eyes,
swishing tail, and claws, etc.), which they manipulate
and – by roaring in unison (with, if possible, a good
deal of amplified help) – they become –

Krindlekrax RAAAAAAAAAAHHHHHHHHHHH!!!!!

Krindlekrax steps towards Ruskin.

Ruskin Leave us alone! This is *my* street! These are *my*
friends!

Krindlekrax RAAAAAHHH!

Ruskin Stop making holes in the road!

Krindlekrax RAAAAAHHH!

Ruskin And cracking the –

Krindlekrax RAAAAAHHH!

Ruskin And burning –

Krindlekrax RAAAAAHHH!

Krindlekrax approaches Ruskin. Its tail swishing, feet
pounding, jaws chomping.

Ruskin runs out of the way.

Ruskin I'm warning you!

Krindlekrax RAAAAAHHH!

Ruskin hits Krindlekrax with his walking stick.

Krindlekrax roars and swishes tail.
Ruskin continues hitting it.

Krindlekrax RAAAAAHHH!

Ruskin Stay in the sewer! Stop bothering us!

The battle between Ruskin and Krindlekrax continues.

Much movement and roaring. The lightning continues to flash. The thunder continues to rumble.

At one point, Ruskin strikes Krindlekrax particularly hard.

Krindlekrax roars in pain.

Elvis disentangles himself from the creature.

Gradually, Ruskin manages to climb up on Krindlekrax. He sits just behind the creature's head, as if it's a bucking bronco.

Ruskin This is *my* street, Krindlekrax!

*Krindlekrax hurls Ruskin from its back.
    Ruskin backs away.*

*Krindlekrax gets closer . . .
    Closer . . .
    Closer . . .
    Then –*

Elvis is seen bouncing his ball, dressed in his night-time clothes (white boxer shorts, black T-shirt) and with his quiffed hair visible. He is sleepwalking.

Ruskin Elvis!

*Krindlekrax stops.
    Then –*

Ruskin Elvis! Get inside! Quick!

Elvis doesn't budge.
   Krindlekrax gets closer.

Ruskin Elvis!

Ruskin tries to push Elvis out of the way.
   Elvis holds his ground, bouncing ball.

Ruskin Move, Elvis! Move!

Bounce . . .
   Bounce . . .

Krindlekrax RAAAAAHHH!

Lightning!
   Thunder!

Bounce!
   Bounce!

Ruskin ELVIS! GO HOME!

Krindlekrax RAAAAAAAHHH!

Krindlekrax is almost on top of them now.
   Ruskin hits Krindlekrax with walking stick.
   He hits the snout.
   Hits . . .
   Hits . . .
   Hits . . .

Krindlekrax pushes Ruskin out of the way.

Ruskin NO!

Throws stick at Krindlekrax.

STOP IT!

Throws helmet.

STOP!

Clutches medal.

Ruskin The medal! A golden medal is like a golden penny . . . I wonder . . .

Krindlekrax RAAAAAHHHHH!

Ruskin Open wide!

Throws medal.

Krindlekrax RAA – !

Medal goes into Krindlekrax's mouth.

Krindlekrax's mouth slams shut.

Krindlekrax freezes.

Pause.

Krindlekrax backs away from Elvis.
It is making painful choking noises.
Slight pause.

Krindlekrax slumps to the ground.
It is whimpering too now.
Slight pause.

Ruskin Wh . . . what happened?

Krindlekrax looks towards Ruskin.
Its whimpering gets louder.

Ruskin Is it the medal?

Krindlekrax opens its mouth.

Ruskin You want me to get the medal out?

Krindlekrax nods.

Ruskin But . . . I . . .

Krindlekrax nods pathetically.

Ruskin Well . . . alright.

Slowly, Ruskin approaches Krindlekrax.
He reaches – or, indeed, crawls – into Krindlekrax's mouth.
He grabs the medal.

Krindlekrax heaves a sigh of relief.

Ruskin stands in front of Krindlekrax and shows the medal.

Ruskin There!

Krindlekrax nuzzles Ruskin affectionately.

Ruskin Will you . . . go back to the sewers?

Krindlekrax nods.

Ruskin And you won't –?

Krindlekrax shakes its head.

Ruskin Goodbye, Krindlekrax.

Krindlekrax nuzzles Ruskin again.
Ruskin strokes its nose.

Krindlekrax makes an almost purring sound.
Then –

Slowly, Krindlekrax walks back to the drain hole.

It climbs back down.

Its tail swishes into the dark until . . .

Krindlekrax is gone.

It starts to rain.

Bounce!

Ruskin Elvis!

Thunder.
Lightning.

Ruskin Elvis. You've got to go home. The weather is –

Thunder!
Lightning!
Rain!
Bounce . . . bounce . . .

Ruskin This way, Elvis. That's it.

*Slowly, shepherded by Ruskin, Elvis makes his way
indoors.*

Ruskin goes round the street . . .

He picks up the walking stick, etc . . .
Then –

Ruskin Pleasant dreams, Lizard Street.

Ruskin gets into bed and –

SCENE NINETEEN: RUSKIN'S BEDROOM

Wendy Get up! Quick! Mr Lace is here! He wants you
to –

Mr Lace Alarum! Alarum!

Rushes in, very flustered, clutching the costume for hero.

Listen! Last night! Elvis! Sleepwalk! Rain! Get up, Ruskin! Up! Up!

Wendy Up!

Ruskin jumps out of bed.

Mr Lace Elvis wakes this morning. Sneezing! Sore throat! Temperature!

Wendy and Mr Lace are dressing Ruskin.

Mr Lace School play! All that work! Now – no hero! . . . Where's the shield?

Wendy Here!

Mr Lace You, Ruskin! You're the only one who can – Sword, sword?

Wendy Here!

Around them – as they prepare Ruskin – everyone else is getting the street ready for the school play: makeshift stage, seats, flags, banners, streamers, etc.

Mr Lace You know what to do, Ruskin. Speak the speeches as – oh, quick! Helmet! – trippingly off the tongue and suit the action to the word and the word to the action and – There! You're ready!

Wendy and Mr Lace admire Ruskin in full costume. Very slight pause.

Wendy You're the hero, Ruskin.

Ruskin picks up Corky's medal and pins it on.

Ruskin . . . I know.

The scene now becomes . . .

SCENE TWENTY: LIZARD STREET

Ruskin is standing on a makeshift stage.

In the dazzling sunlight the street looks glorious; flags (with the red-eyed, green-skinned dragon against sky blue), red-green-sky-blue streamers and banners, etc., and a huge sign with the name of the play.

On stage with Ruskin is a (none too convincing) cardboard and chicken-wire dragon (bright green with red eyes). It is being operated by a none-too-proficient Mr Lace.

Wendy, Winston, Dr Flowers, Mr Flick, Mrs Walnut, Mr Cave and Mrs Cave are all sitting in front of stage, avidly watching the play as it draws to its thrilling conclusion.

Ruskin 'Stay back, Dragon! I am not afraid! I am handsome and strong! Look at my muscles! Listen to my voice – like thunder!'

Mr Lace (*as Dragon*) Snarlumph.

Mr Cave Chop its head off!

Mrs Cave Yeah! Do it!

It's quite clear that Mr Cave and Mrs Cave – like all the others – have been totally engrossed in the play.

protect them. Go back to your cave, Dragon. Don't ever threaten this place again . . . Take that! And that!'

Mr Lace Snarlumph.

Ruskin 'I will not let you beat me, Dragon. I am Young Hal Oaktree. And this is my home . . . this is my home . . . Hear me? My home!'

Looks round.

(*in stage whisper*) Where's Sparkey?

Mr Lace (*in stage whisper*) Sparkey! Quick! You're on!

Sparkey rushes onto stage, wearing blonde wig and dress. He is obviously uncomfortable and embarrassed but trying his best. When he speaks it's a high-pitched attempt at 'damsel in distress'.

Sparkey 'Oooo! Help! Young Hal Oaktree! Don't let the Dragon get me!'

Ruskin stabs at cardboard Dragon. The Dragon seems to be winning, beating Ruskin back. In desperation Ruskin throws his sword at the Dragon. Then he throws his helmet. Then he takes a large golden penny from his pocket.

Ruskin 'The golden penny the Wizard gave me for helping him!'

Throws penny.

The penny goes into the Dragon's mouth. Dragon makes a choking noise (Mr Lace is hamming terribly) and collapses to the ground.

Ruskin grabs sword and raises it for fatal blow.

Mr Cave Do it!

Mrs Cave Do it!

*Everyone urges him on.
But –*

Ruskin No.

Mr Lace No? . . . (*in stage whisper*) Ruskin! The script!
You cut the Dragon's head off . . . Ruskin? Head! Chop!

Ruskin You're in pain, Dragon. Let me remove the
penny from your throat.

> *Mr Lace hesitates a moment, baffled. Then, not
> knowing what else to do, he opens the Dragon's
> mouth.*

> *Ruskin removes the penny.*

> *The audience 'oooos' and 'ahhhhs', obviously gripped
> by this surprising turn of events.*

Ruskin Now, listen, Dragon.

> *Slight pause*

You listening?

> *Mr Lace hastily – and in a very confused state – nods
> Dragon's head.*

Ruskin There's no reason we can't all live together. Look
what our battle has done to the countryside . . . Do it
now, Sparkey!

Mr Lace Sparkey! Your speech!

Sparkey 'So . . . oh, Young Hal Oaktree, how brave you

Ruskin That's right, Ophelia! From now on, this village
will grow and prosper. It will be a community of

harmony and peace. This earth of majesty, this other
Eden, demi-paradise, this fortress built by Nature for
herself, this is our own little world, this blessed plot, this
realm . . . this Lizard Street!'

*Everyone cheers and claps. None more so than
Mr and Mrs Cave. All seem to be a little watery-eyed.
The applause is deafening as –*

*Elvis appears – in black dressing gown – bouncing
ball. His nose is red with the chill he caught in last
night's rain.*

*Gradually, everyone becomes aware of Elvis.
The applause grinds to a halt.
Silence.
Pause.*

Mr Cave Now, son. No trouble.

Mrs Cave You had a fever, Elvey-baby.

Mr Cave A sore throat.

Mrs Cave We tried to get Mr Lace to postpone.

Mr Lace But I couldn't, Elvis.

Mr Cave Wasn't possible.

Mrs Cave Ruskin came to the rescue.

Mr Lace He was the only one who could.

Mr Cave And Elvis . . . Ruskin was good.

Wendy More than good.

Mr Flick Oscar-winning!

Mr Lace Worthy of William Shakes –

All (*except Elvis and Ruskin*) Don't say it!

Elvis bounces ball.
  Others watch in silence.
  Pause.

Slowly, Elvis approaches makeshift stage.
  Elvis climbs on stage and faces Ruskin.
  Elvis stops bouncing ball.
  Slight pause.

Elvis I watched you from my window.

Ruskin . . . Oh.

Elvis You were brilliant.

Ruskin . . . Thanks.

Elvis Better than I could do it.

The others are now clustered round stage, watching Ruskin and Elvis as if it were a new play (and reacting with 'ooo's and 'ahhh's and ripples of applause, etc.).

Elvis I spoke to Corky first, you know.

Ruskin That's right. You did.

Elvis I . . . I wanted him to be my friend.

Ruskin He wanted that too.

Elvis No, he didn't.

Sparkey And me!

Ruskin All of us. But *you* . . . you got jealous, Elvis. When Corky and me started to talk about acting and theatre and stuff, you stormed off.

Elvis . . . I don't know anything about all of that.

Ruskin You could've tried.

Elvis You didn't *want* me to try.

Ruskin That's not true!

Elvis It is!

Ruskin No!

Sparkey I think . . . I think it's a little bit true, Rusk. I think . . . I think you liked having Corky all to yourself.

Slight pause.

Ruskin Well . . . perhaps I did.

Elvis indicates football.

Elvis Corky bought this for you.

Ruskin He wanted us all to play with it, though.

Sparkey That's right. He did.

Elvis But I got jealous and stole it and used it to –

Ruskin stabs football with pin on medal.
The ball explodes with a deafening –

BANG!

Everyone gasps.
Slight pause.

Elvis I . . . I didn't want muscles. I didn't want a deep voice. I didn't want to be this tall. Why's it happened to me? So fast and . . . Every day is like a ghost train.

Ruskin But Elvis . . . there's nothing to be scared of.

Slight pause.

Elvis I had . . . this strange dream last night. You were in it and . . . you saved me from . . . something. I don't know what it was, But . . . you saved me and . . . and . . .

Slight pause.

I miss Corky.

Ruskin Me too.

Elvis Can we . . . talk about him?

Ruskin Much as you like.

Ruskin and Elvis embrace.

Everyone claps and cheers.
   It is a real celebration: party poppers, balloons, ticker tape.
   Then . . . out of this euphoria –

Wendy (*singing*)
   'And did that hero Hal Oaktree
   Battle a Dragon where we stand?'

Wendy lets her coat fall to the ground. The dress beneath is now revealed: a dazzling, green-sequinned number.

. . . *smacked wonder.*

And in this place our . . .
And blaze with pride both day and night

For we are living in Lizard Street
And Lizard Street lives inside us.'

*As the song builds, Corky appears onstage behind
everyone. The others, of course, do not see him . . .
but he is there, part of the street, as the song reaches
its triumphant conclusion.*

All (*singing*)
'Sing we the joys of Lizard Street.
Sing we of friendship brave and true.
Sing we of life like burnished gold.
Sing we of wonderment untold.
I have no need to roam or stray
For here I've found my family.
And so I'll stay in Paradise.
For Lizard Street's my dest – in – y!'

Ruskin (*overlapping end of song*) I LOVE YOU,
LIZARD STREET! I LOVE YOU!

Blackout.